BTEC Level 3 National Study Skills Guide in Eng...

Welcome to your Study Skills Guide! ... make it your own – start by adding your personal and course details below...

Learner's name: _____

BTEC course title: _____

Date started: _____

Mandatory units:

_____

_____

_____

Optional units:

_____

_____

_____

_____

Centre name: _____

Centre address:

_____

_____

_____

Tutor's name: _____

Published by Pearson Education Limited, a company incorporated in England and Wales, having its registered office at Edinburgh Gate, Harlow, Essex, CM20 2JE. Registered company number: 872828

Edexcel is a registered trademark of Edexcel Limited

Text © Pearson Education Limited 2010

First published 2010

19   18

21

British Library Cataloguing in Publication Data

A catalogue record for this book is available from the British Library

ISBN 978 1 84690 559 9

Typeset and edited by DSM Partnership
Cover design by Visual Philosophy, created by eMC Design
Cover photo/illustration © Corbis: Bill Varie
Printed and bound by L.E.G.O. S.p.A. Lavis (TN) - Italy

Acknowledgements

The author and publisher would like to thank the following individuals and organisations for permission to reproduce photographs:

Alamy Images: David R. Frazier Photolibrary, Inc 7, Angela Hampton Picture Library 19, Claudia Wiens 60; Corbis: 72; Getty Images: Bloomberg 10; iStockphoto: Chris Schmidt 33; Pearson Education Ltd: Steve Shott 28, Ian Wedgewood 53.

All other images © Pearson Education

Every effort has been made to contact copyright holders of material reproduced in this book. Any omissions will be rectified in subsequent printings if notice is given to the publishers.

Websites

Go to www.pearsonhotlinks.co.uk to gain access to the relevant website links and information on how they can aid your studies. When you access the site, search for either the title BTEC Level 3 National Study Skills Guide in Engineering or the ISBN 978184605599.

Disclaimer

This material has been published on behalf of Edexcel and offers high-quality support for the delivery of Edexcel qualifications.

This does not mean that the material is essential to achieve any Edexcel qualification, nor does it mean that it is the only suitable material available to support any Edexcel qualification. Edexcel material will not be used verbatim in setting any Edexcel examination or assessment. Any resource lists produced by Edexcel shall include this and other appropriate resources.

Copies of official specifications for all Edexcel qualifications may be found on the Edexcel website: www.edexcel.com

Contents

Popular progression pathways

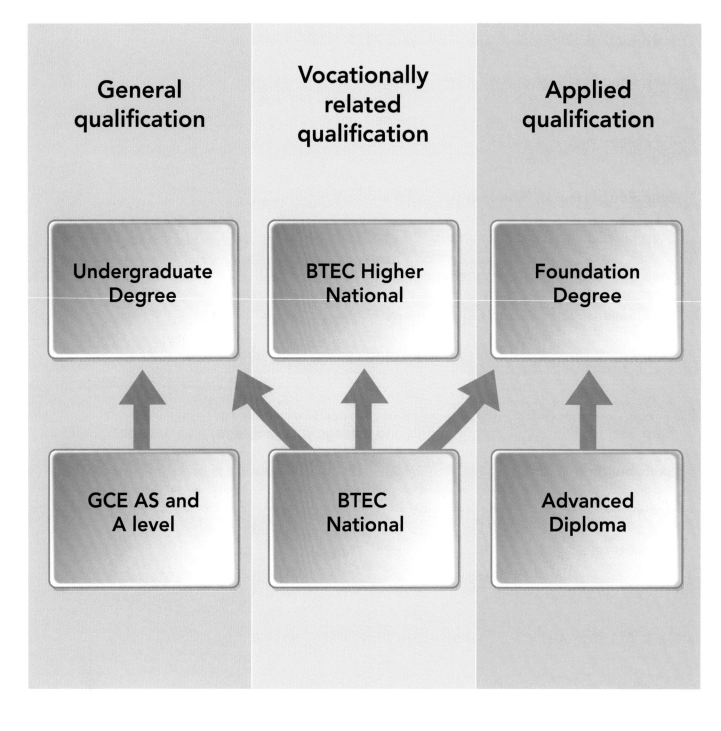

Ten steps to success in your BTEC Level 3 National

This Study Skills Guide has been written to help you achieve the best result possible on your BTEC Level 3 National course. At the start of a new course you may feel both quite excited and also a little apprehensive. Taking a BTEC Level 3 National qualification has many benefits and is a major stepping stone towards your future career. Using this Study Skills Guide will help you get the most out of your course from the start.

TOP TIP

Use this Study Skills Guide at your own pace. Dip in to find what you need. Look back at it whenever you have a problem or query.

During **induction** sessions at the start of your course your tutor will explain important information, but it can be difficult to remember everything, and that's when you'll find this Study Skills Guide invaluable. Look at it whenever you want to check anything related to your course. It provides all the essential facts you need and has a Useful terms section to explain specialist terms, words and phrases, including some that you will see highlighted in this book in bold type.

This Study Skills Guide covers the skills you'll need to do well in your course – such as managing your time, researching and analysing information, and preparing a presentation.

- Use the **Top tips** to make your life easier as you go.
- Use the **Key points** to help you to stay focused on the essentials.
- Use the **Action points** to check what you need to know or do now.
- Use the **Case studies** to relate information to your chosen sector and vocational area.

- Use the **Activities** to test your knowledge and skills.
- Use the **Useful terms** section to check the meaning of specialist terms.

This Study Skills Guide has been designed to work alongside the Edexcel Student Book for BTEC Level 3 National Engineering (Edexcel, 2010). This Student Book includes the main knowledge you'll need, with tips from BTEC experts, Edexcel assignment tips, assessment activities and up-to-date case studies from industry experts, plus handy references to your Study Skills Guide.

This Study Skills Guide is divided into ten steps, each relating to a key aspect of your studies, from understanding assessment to time management to maximising opportunities. Concentrate on getting things right one step at a time. Thousands of learners have achieved BTEC Level 3 National qualifications and are now studying for a degree, or building a successful career at work. Using this Study Skills Guide, and believing in your own abilities, will help you achieve your future goals, too.

Introduction to the engineering sector

Engineering is a really great industry to be involved with because of its diverse nature, which is reflected in the different strands of the Level 3 National programme. You will notice in this guide that reference is made to:

- mechanical engineering
- manufacturing engineering
- operations and maintenance engineering
- electrical and electronic engineering
- aerospace engineering.

What type of job could one of these qualifications lead to? This is a difficult question to answer in a limited space. So, let's start by thinking about some examples of people who work in engineering.

Where do you see yourself when you have achieved your Level 3 National qualification? You may look to work as a technician, although if you have really good craft skills then you might wish to become a craftsperson.

To get to be an engineer you will need a higher level qualification, such as a Higher Diploma, which you can take after completing your Level 3 National. This would be followed up, perhaps, by a degree in engineering, and registration with a professional body.

One thing to be clear about is that without engineers life as we know it would cease to exist. Everything we do or touch involves products that have been designed, manufactured or installed by engineers. Many simple everyday products contain complex engineering. For example, a

drinks can is made from extremely thin metal that holds liquid at high pressure, with a pull tab that must work every time. At the other extreme, think about the latest generation of mobile phones, computers and games consoles.

'Crazy scientists' or inventors may come up with wacky ideas, but it is engineers who turn those ideas into reality. Each year the big car manufacturers display concept vehicles that have cost millions to develop. Engineers take these ideas, simplify them and set up mass production systems that allow cars to be built and sold for an affordable price.

If you read newspapers or watch television, you may see commentators predicting the demise of engineering in this country. There has been, and will continue to be, a trend in manufacturing industry for design and development functions to remain in the UK, with production outsourced to economies with lower wage costs. But what happens when, as is currently happening in the Far East, wage costs abroad begin to rise? Be

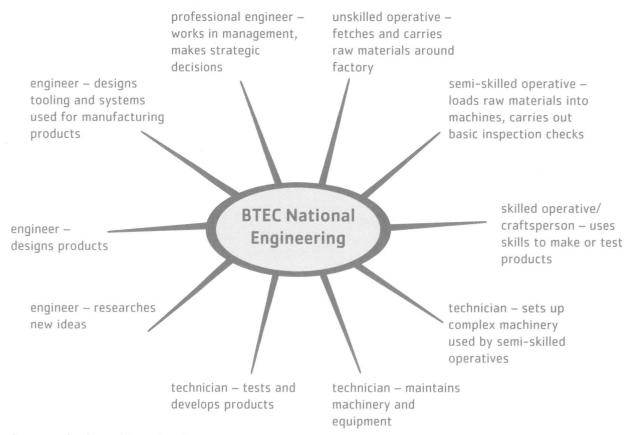

Some people who work in engineering

Without engineers, you wouldn't be reading this book!

assured that your time spent studying for an engineering qualification will not be wasted. People want state-of-the-art products, and there are many challenges remaining to be solved in fields such as medical science, sustainability and environmental engineering, and communications technology.

What will you learn about on the course?

Irrespective of which strand of engineering you are interested in, there are four important common elements:

- safety in the workplace
- effective communication
- project management
- mathematical modelling of problems.

Everything else hangs off these mandatory topics. The other subjects you will study are customised to match the requirements of the particular strand that you're following.

As you go through your studies, you'll discover that successful engineering businesses invariably get things right first time. To achieve this goal, the people working in the industry must have expert knowledge. Now is your chance to become one of those experts!

Skills for your sector

People who work in engineering use a wide range of skills. This is demonstrated in the following case study.

Case study: Using specialised engineering skills

Liam works for DomProd Ltd. He is a project engineer responsible for the design and development of a new product. This has recently gone on sale in major electrical retailers such as Comet and Currys. The production version of the product was factory-tested against specification, and it was certified as fit for purpose and compliant with British and European standards. The product has several components including an electronic circuit board, cooling fan, plastic outer casing, electric motor and switches.

Cara is the quality assurance manager at DomProd Ltd. She has received a lot of phone calls from retailers reporting problems with the product. Customers have been returning the product because of an overheating problem that occurs after several hours' use. The retailers have carried out checks and cannot identify the cause of the problem, but they confirm that it can be quite severe. One customer is claiming that the plastic casing became so hot that her young child burnt his hand when he touched it. There is talk of legal action, and Trading Standards may become involved.

Liam is very concerned because, as far as he is aware, the design calculations are accurate and the correct cooling fans and motors have been delivered by a subcontractor.

He calls a meeting with the following staff:

- the designer who did the calculations and detailed design work
- the person responsible for ordering components from subcontractors
- the production manager
- the test and certification manager
- the quality assurance manager, Cara
- a lawyer from the legal department
- the sales manager.

The skills that Liam uses in the meeting mirror those that you will develop on the course.

First, there are the specialised engineering skills that he needs in order to be able to:

- interpret the technical specification for the product
- interpret technical drawings presented within a CAD package
- understand data that the test and certification manager will present
- understand quality assurance data relating to the manufacture of the product
- make suggestions about any design modifications that may be needed
- assess the affect of the problem on DomProd's reputation and profitability
- evaluate all the information presented at the meeting and produce an action plan for resolving the problem.

Second, Liam will be using generic skills that apply to any type of job and which you will also develop on the course. These include English, ICT and maths functional skills and the six personal, learning and thinking skills (PLTS):

1 **Independent enquirer** (IE) – identifying the cause of the problem.
2 **Creative thinker** (CT) – investigating ways to resolve the problem.
3 **Reflective learner** (RL) – reviewing decisions taken at the meeting at some future date.
4 **Team worker** (TW) – working in a team.
5 **Self-manager** (SM) – prioritising actions.
6 **Effective participator** (EP) – proposing at the meeting a practical way forward to resolve the problem.

There is an interaction between technical skills and generic skills – the skills are applicable to any type of job, not just to engineering. For example, if Liam ever decided to change to a different profession, his generic skills move with him: they are portable. This is important in a labour market with ever-increasing mobility.

Reflection point

What about the other people at the meeting – what skills will they use?

Step One: Understand your course and how it works

Case study: Where could the BTEC National in Engineering take you?

When he was at secondary school, Jeff did well in mathematics, science, and design and technology. He decided to continue his education at a further education college, and last September enrolled on a BTEC Level 3 Subsidiary Diploma in Engineering as well as taking AS levels in mathematics and design and technology. At that time, Jeff was unsure about his career aspirations and wanted to keep his options open. He liked being able to accumulate an individual record of credit for each of the units studied on the BTEC.

One of Jeff's assignments involved getting information about a career pathway from a senior design engineer at a local company. The designer explained that she went straight from school into an apprenticeship with the company, and she went on to take BTEC National and Higher Nationals in electronic engineering. At the time of her meeting with Jeff she was halfway through a part-time BSc in microelectronic systems design.

'What Kate told me was really interesting, and I've decided to apply for a mechanical engineering apprenticeship with her company. I've discussed my career objectives with my tutor and, if I get the apprenticeship, he is very agreeable to me moving on to the 120-credit National Diploma next September. This will take a year to complete as a part-time student, and the credits I accumulate for it, together with the AS levels I'm doing, will set me up nicely for a Higher National.

'Kate told me how important it is to develop other skills to support my engineering knowledge, particularly personal, learning and thinking skills. She said that as a design engineer she has to get things done on time, and be able to make presentations to customers and other people in the company.

'Kate admitted that when she started her apprenticeship she was very nervous about putting her point of view forward, making decisions and standing up in front of people. The BTEC system of teaching, learning and assessment helped her develop these skills, which I think is great.

'Another thing that impressed me about Kate is her level of responsibility – she is managing a £1 million design project and she's not yet 30. And what a great car she drives!'

Reflection point

What do you think the benefits might be of studying and working at the same time?

All BTEC Level 3 National qualifications are **vocational** or **work-related**. This means that you gain specific knowledge and understanding relevant to your chosen area. It gives you several advantages when you start work. For example, you will already know quite a lot about your chosen area, which will help you settle down more quickly. If you are already employed in a full- or part-time job, you become more valuable to your employer.

Your BTEC course will prepare you for the work you want to do.

There are four types of BTEC Level 3 National qualification: Certificates, Subsidiary Diplomas, Diplomas and Extended Diplomas

	Certificate	Subsidiary Diploma	Diploma	Extended Diploma
Credit	30	60	120	180
Equivalence	1 AS level	1 A level	2 A levels	3 A levels

These qualifications are often described as **nested**. This means that they fit inside each other (rather like Russian dolls) because the same units are common to each qualification – so you can progress from one to another easily by completing more units.

TOP TIP

The structure of BTEC Level 3 National qualifications means it's easy to progress from one type to another and gain more credits, as well as to specialise in particular areas that interest you.

- Every BTEC Level 3 National qualification has a set number of **mandatory units** that all learners must complete.
- All BTEC Level 3 National qualifications include **optional units** that enable you to study particular areas in more depth.

- Some BTEC Level 3 National qualifications have **specialist pathways**, which may have additional mandatory units. These specialist pathways allow you to follow your career aims more precisely. For example, if you are studying to become an IT practitioner, you can choose pathways in software development, networking, systems support, or IT and business.

- On all BTEC courses you are expected to be responsible for your own learning. Obviously your tutor will give you help and guidance when necessary, but you also need to be 'self-starting' and able to use your own initiative. Ideally, you can also assess how well you are doing and make improvements when necessary.

- BTEC Level 3 National grades convert to UCAS points, just like A levels, but the way you are assessed and graded on a BTEC course is different, as you will see in the next section.

Key points

- You can study part-time or full-time for your BTEC Level 3 National.

- You can do a Certificate, Subsidiary Diploma, Diploma or Extended Diploma, and progress easily from one to the other.

- You will study both mandatory units and optional units on your course.

- When you have completed your BTEC course you can get a job (or **apprenticeship**), use your qualification to develop your career and/or continue studying to degree level.

- On all BTEC Level 3 National courses, the majority of your learning is practical and vocationally focused to develop the skills you need for your chosen career.

Using the Edexcel website to find out about your course

- You can check all the details about your BTEC Level 3 National course on the Edexcel website – go to www.edexcel.com.

- Enter the title of your BTEC Level 3 National qualification in the qualifications finder.

- Now find the specification in the list of documents. This is a long document so don't try to print it. Instead, look at the information on the units you will be studying to see the main topics you will cover.

- Then save the document or bookmark the page so that you can easily refer to it again if you need to.

Action points

1 By discussing with your tutor and by exploring the Edexcel website, find out the key information about your course and use it to complete the 'Important information' form on the next page. You can refer to this form at any time to refresh your memory about any part of your studies.

a) Check whether you are studying for a BTEC Level 3 Certificate, Subsidiary Diploma, Diploma, or Extended Diploma, and find out the number of units you will be studying.

b) Find out the titles of the mandatory units you will be studying.

c) Find out the titles of the optional units and identify the ones offered at your centre.

d) Check the length of your course, and when you will be studying each unit.

e) Identify the optional units you will be taking. On some National courses you will do this at the start, while on others you may make your final decision later.

f) Find out other relevant information about your BTEC Level 3 National qualification. Your centre may have already given you details about the course structure.

g) Ask your tutor to help you to complete section 10 on the form. Depending on your course, you may be developing specific additional or personal skills – such as personal, learning and thinking skills (PLTS) and functional skills – or spending time on work experience, going on visits or doing other activities linked to your subject area.

h) Talk to your tutor about section 12 on the form, as your sources of information will depend on the careers guidance and information at your centre. You may find it useful to exchange ideas with other members of your class.

	IMPORTANT INFORMATION ON MY BTEC LEVEL 3 NATIONAL COURSE
1	The title of the BTEC Level 3 National qualification I am studying is:
2	The length of my course is:
3	The total number of units I will study is:
4	The number of mandatory units I have to study is:
5	The titles of these mandatory units and the dates (or terms) when I will study them are:
6	The main topics I will learn in each mandatory unit include:

	IMPORTANT INFORMATION ON MY BTEC LEVEL 3 NATIONAL COURSE
7	The number of optional units I have to study is:
8	The titles of the optional units I will study are:
9	The main topics I will learn in each optional unit include:
10	Other important aspects of my course are:
11	After I have achieved my BTEC Level 3 National my options include:
12	Useful sources of information I can use to find out more about these options include:

2 Many learners already have information, contacts or direct experiences that relate to their course. For example, you may have a specific interest or hobby that links to a unit, such as being a St John Ambulance cadet if you are studying Public Services. Think about the relevant sources of information you already have access to and complete the table below.

MY INFORMATION SOURCES	
Experts I know	(Who they are, what they know)
My hobbies and interests	(What they are, what they involve)
My job(s)	(Past and present work and work experience, and what I did)
Programmes I like to watch	(What these are, how they relate to my course)

Magazines and/or books I read	(What these are, examples of relevant articles)
ICT sources	(My centre's intranet as well as useful websites)
Other	(Other sources relevant for my particular course and the topics I will be studying)

Activity: Your future options

At the start of a new course it is important to begin to think about what options may be available to you as you consider a future career in engineering. On page 5 of this guide there is a list of some of the different engineering sectors, such as aerospace and manufacturing, and on page 6 there is a mind map of job roles associated with engineering.

What do you hope to be doing in, say, five years' time, and how do you achieve this goal? What practical and technical skills will you need to pick up along the way? What happens if, as you progress with your studies and training, your career aspirations change?

Create a mind map to explore the range of career options available to you in engineering and the routes to success. For example, if you wish to work in a design environment, then explore the routes to becoming a member of the Institution of Engineering Designers.

A good starting point is the website of the Sector Skills Council for Science, Engineering and Manufacturing Technologies (SEMTA). There is information on engineering careers and qualifications. Go to page 94 to find out how to access a useful website for this activity.

Use the space on the following page to record your ideas.

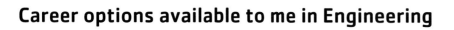
Career options available to me in Engineering

Step Two: Understand how you are assessed and graded

Case study: Combining GCSEs and BTECs

When she was at secondary school, Kalpa combined GCSEs with a BTEC First in Engineering. She really enjoyed the subjects but was never too sure about how the final grades would be worked out. Her tutor told her not to worry, that 'everything will turn out fine, just concentrate on your subjects, follow our guidance and hand in your portfolios of work on time'. Kalpa got good results and so she decided to do a BTEC Level 3 Extended Diploma at the local further education college, as this could lead to a place at university or to further studies at the college.

The course brochure contained information about unit content, assessment, grades, points, learning skills and monitoring progress, but Kalpa was determined to do very well on the course, so she arranged a meeting with the programme manager to establish exactly how she would be assessed and graded. She wanted to get the best possible result for her two years of hard work.

'The programme manager was very helpful. He said that, although it seems complicated, once you learn how the BTEC assessment system works it is really quite straightforward. The important thing is to keep track of where you are. You need a good filing system for keeping your assignments and recording the grades awarded. All units are assessed internally, in small chunks of work. I like this system because I find big exams a bit daunting.'

Kalpa did well on her Extended Diploma, and she achieved her expected unit and qualification grades. She received offers of university places through the UCAS system. However, she decided against university and took up a technician apprenticeship with an engineering company. Her BTEC National qualification grade gave her entry onto a foundation degree programme, which she studies part-time. Kalpa is now coming towards the end of her apprenticeship and works in her company's product testing laboratory.

Reflection points

How do you start earning points (credits) from day one?

At the end of the course will you feel that all the effort has been worthwhile?

Your assessment

This section looks at the importance of your assignments, how they are graded and how this converts into unit points and UCAS points. Unlike A-levels, there are no externally-set final exams on a BTEC course. Even if you know this because you already have a BTEC First qualification, you should still read this section, as now you will be working at a different level.

Your learning is assessed by **assignments**, set by your tutors. You will complete these throughout your course, using many different **assessment methods**, such as real-life case studies, **projects** and presentations. Some assignments may be work-based or **time-constrained** – it depends very much on the vocational area you are studying.

Your assignments are based on **learning outcomes** set by Edexcel. These are listed for each unit in your course specification. You must achieve **all** the learning outcomes to pass each unit.

TOP TIP

Check the learning outcomes for each unit by referring to the course specification – go to www.edexcel.com.

Important skills to help you achieve your grades include:

- researching and analysing information (see page 57)
- using your time effectively (see page 25)
- working cooperatively as a member of a team (see page 51.)

Your grades, unit points and UCAS points

On a BTEC Level 3 National course, assessments that meet the learning outcomes are graded as pass, merit or distinction. The different grades within each unit are set out by Edexcel as **grading criteria** in a **grading grid**. These criteria identify the **higher-level skills** you must demonstrate to achieve a higher grade (see also Step Six: Understand your assessment, on page 35).

All your assessment grades earn **unit points**. The total points you get for all your units determine your final qualification grade(s) – pass, merit or distinction. You get:

- one final grade if you are taking a Certificate or Subsidiary Diploma
- two final grades if you are taking a Diploma
- three final grades if you are taking an Extended Diploma.

Your points and overall grade(s) convert to **UCAS points**, which you need to be accepted onto a degree course. For example, if you achieve three final pass grades for your BTEC Level 3 Extended Diploma, you get 120 UCAS Tariff points. If you achieve three final distinction grades, this increases to 360 – equivalent to three GCE A-levels.

Please note that all UCAS information was correct at the time of going to print, but we would advise that you check the UCAS website for the most up to date information. See page 94 for how to access their website.

Case study: Securing a university place

Chris and Shaheeda both want a university place and have worked hard on their BTEC Level 3 Extended Diploma course.

Chris's final score is 226 unit points, which converts to 280 UCAS Tariff points. Shaheeda has a total score of 228 unit points – just two points more – which converts to 320 UCAS points! This is because a score of between 204 and 227 unit points gives 280 UCAS points, whereas a score of 228 to 251 points gives 320 UCAS points.

Shaheeda is delighted because this increases her chances of getting a place on the degree course she wants. Chris is annoyed. He says if he had realised, he would have worked harder on his last assignment to get two more points.

You start to earn points from your first assessment, so you get many benefits from settling in quickly and doing good work from the start. Understanding how **grade boundaries** work also helps you to focus your efforts to get the best possible final grade.

You will be able to discuss your learning experiences, your personal progress and the achievement of your learning objectives in **individual tutorials** with your tutor. These enable you to monitor your progress and overcome temporary difficulties. You can also talk about any worries you have. Your tutor is one of your most important resources, and a tutorial gives you their undivided attention.

You can talk through any questions or problems in your tutorials.

Key points

- Your learning is assessed in a variety of ways, such as by assignments, projects and real-life case studies.

- You need to demonstrate specific knowledge and skills to achieve the learning outcomes set by Edexcel. You must achieve all the grading criteria to pass a unit.

- The grading criteria for pass, merit and distinction are shown in a grading grid for the unit. Higher-level skills are needed for higher grades.

- The assessment grades of pass, merit and distinction convert to unit points. The total unit points you receive for the course determine your final overall grade(s) and UCAS points.

TOP TIP

It's always tempting to spend longer on work you like doing and are good at, but focusing on improving your weak areas will do more to boost your overall grade(s).

Action points

1 Find out more about your own course by carrying out this activity.

a) Find the learning outcomes for the units you are currently studying. Your tutor may have given you these, or you can find them in your course specification – go to www.edexcel.com.

b) Look at the grading grid for the units and identify the way the requirements change for the higher grades. If there are some unfamiliar words, check these in Step Six of this guide (see page 35 onwards).

c) If the unit points system still seems complicated, ask your tutor to explain it.

d) Check the UCAS points you would need for the course or university which interests you.

e) Design a form you can use to record the unit points you earn throughout your course. Keep this up to date. Regularly check how your points relate to your overall grade(s), based on the grade boundaries for your qualification. Your tutor can give you this information or you can check it yourself in the course specification.

Activity: Assessment and grading

To see how well you have grasped the main issues about assessment, try to answer these questions about the BTEC Level 3 National in Engineering.

How many different ways can you think of producing evidence of learning for an assignment? For example, one way you can demonstrate your learning is through a PowerPoint presentation.

What are the four learning outcomes for Unit 1?

Engineering units have grading grid statements that start with a key word such as identify, describe, explain and justify. What is the link between the key words and the pass, merit and distinction grading criteria?

Why do you think it is important to fully understand how the BTEC Level National in Engineering is structured, how you are assessed and graded, and what are your possible progression routes?

Having read through this section dealing with how you are assessed and graded, list any areas that remain unclear. Make a point of discussing these points with your tutor to resolve any issues.

Step Three: Understand yourself

Case study: Being self-aware

David didn't really enjoy secondary school because he found it hard to make friends, and he was regarded as something of a loner. Quiet and reserved in class, he had difficulty taking part in group discussions despite the encouragement of his tutors. However, David got on really well with his technology tutor, and it was she who suggested that he might benefit from carrying out a self-awareness review.

'Look at it this way,' she said, 'we all have strengths and we all have weaknesses. Teaching in the classroom is not a problem for me, but can you remember the first time I took full school assembly? The head really dropped me in it – just 15 minutes' warning! I was terrified and realised that being nervous of talking to a large audience was a weakness I had to overcome.'

The technology tutor went on to explain to David how he could carry out a self-awareness review to identify his skills, abilities, strengths and weaknesses. This review would be a good starting point for a personal action plan.

'Talking to my technology tutor really helped me with my BTEC National course – particularly with developing and tracking PLTS. When I started on the course I was not sure whether I would be able to cope with teamwork activities. However, I was surprised and relieved to discover that several other people on the course also found it difficult to contribute to team activities!

'One of my strengths is being able to sit down and really think through a problem before presenting a solution. This has got me really interested in engineering design. People listen and take notice of you if you are well prepared.'

Reflection points

Think about your strengths and weaknesses when you are in a classroom situation:

- What might be a weakness that you have?
- How can you work on it to improve?
- What do you think is your main strength?
- How can you put this strength to good use?

Self-awareness means understanding how you 'tick'. For example, do you prefer practical activities rather than theory? Do you prefer to draw or sketch an idea, rather than write about it?

Self-awareness is important as it makes you less reliant on other people's opinions and gives you confidence in your own judgement. You can also reflect on your actions to learn from your experiences.

Self-awareness also means knowing your own strengths and weaknesses. Knowing your strengths enables you to feel positive and confident about yourself and your abilities. Knowing your weaknesses means you know the areas you need to develop.

You can analyse yourself by looking at...

... your personality and preferences

You may have taken a personality test at your centre. If not, your tutor may recommend one to use, or there are many available online.

Many employers ask job candidates to complete a personality test so that they can match the type of work they are offering to the most suitable people. Although these tests can only give a broad indication of someone's personality, they may help to avoid mismatches, such as hiring someone who is introverted to work in sales.

... your skills and abilities

To succeed in your assignments and to progress in a career requires a number of skills. Some may be vocationally specific, or professional, skills that you can improve during your course – such as sporting performance on a Sports course. Others are broader skills that are invaluable no matter what you are studying – such as communicating clearly and cooperating with others.

You will work faster and more accurately, and have greater confidence, if you are skilled and proficient. A quick skills check will identify any problem areas.

TOP TIP

Use the Skills building section on page 83 to identify the skills you need for your course. You'll also find hints and tips for improving any weak areas.

Key points

- You need certain skills and abilities to get the most out of your BTEC Level 3 National course and to develop your career potential.
- Knowing your strengths and weaknesses is a sign of maturity. It gives you greater confidence in your abilities and enables you to focus on areas for improvement.

TOP TIP

You will find more help in this guide on developing your skills in using time wisely (Step Four), working as a member of a group (Step Seven), researching and analysing information (Step Eight) and making effective presentations (Step Nine).

Action points

1 Gain insight into your own personality by ticking **True** or **False** against each of the following statements. Be honest!

		True	False
a)	If someone annoys me, I can tell them about it without causing offence.		
b)	If someone is talking, I often interrupt them to give them my opinion.		
c)	I get really stressed if I'm under pressure.		
d)	I can sometimes become very emotional and upset on other people's behalf.		
e)	I sometimes worry that I can't cope and may make a mess of something.		
f)	I am usually keen, enthusiastic and motivated to do well.		
g)	I enjoy planning and organising my work.		
h)	I find it easy to work and cooperate with other people and take account of their opinions.		
i)	I am easily influenced by other people.		
j)	I often jump to conclusions and judge people and situations on first impressions.		
k)	I prefer to rely on facts and experience rather than following my instincts.		

Now identify which of the skills and qualities in the box below will be really important in your chosen career.

> tact   truthfulness   listening skills
> **staying calm under pressure**
> **empathy with others**   **self-confidence**
> **initiative**   **planning and organising**
> **working with others**   **self-assurance**
> **objective judgements**

Use your answers to identify areas you should work on to be successful in the future.

2 As part of the UCAS process, all **higher education** applicants have to write a personal statement. This is different from a CV, which is a summary of achievements that all job applicants prepare. You may have already prepared a CV but not thought about a personal statement. Now is your chance!

Read the information about personal statements in the box. Then answer these questions:

a) Explain why personal statements are so important for higher education applicants.

b) Why do you think it is important for your personal statement to read well and be error-free?

c) Suggest three reasons why you shouldn't copy a pre-written statement you have found online.

d) Check the websites you can access from the hotlink given in the box to see what to include in the statement and how to set it out.

e) Prepare a bullet point list of ten personal facts. Focus on your strengths and good reasons why you should be given a place on the higher education course of your choice. If possible, discuss your list with your tutor. Then keep it safe, as it will be useful if you need to write a personal statement later.

Personal statements

This is the information that all higher education applicants have to put in the blank space on their UCAS form. The aim is to sell yourself to admissions tutors. It can be pretty scary, especially if you haven't written anything like it before.

So, where do you start?

First, **never** copy pre-written statements you find online. These are just for guidance. Even worse are websites that offer to write your statement for a fee, and send you a few general, pre-written paragraphs. Forget them all: you can do better!

Imagine you are an admissions tutor with 60 places to offer to 200 applicants. What will you need to read in a personal statement to persuade you to offer the applicant a place?

Most likely, clear explanations about:
- what the applicant can contribute to the course
- why the applicant really wants a place on your course
- what the applicant has done to further his/her own interests in this area, such as voluntary work
- attributes that show this applicant would be a definite bonus – such as innovative ideas, with evidence eg 'I organised a newsletter which we published every three months …'

A personal statement should be well written, with no grammatical or spelling errors, and organised into clear paragraphs.

For further guidance on personal statements, go to page 94 to find out how to access a number of helpful websites.

Activity: Preparing your personal statement

Your research into higher education degree courses has identified several universities that offer the BSc (Hons) in Mechanical Design and Manufacture (UCAS code HH37). You particularly like the look of the course offered by the University of Plymouth. (Go to page 94 to find out how to access the web page for this course.) In addition, living in Plymouth would allow you to continue enjoying your hobby of diving to and exploring underwater structures.

Using the ten personal facts you identified in the bullet list you prepared for point **e)** on page 23, plan a UCAS personal statement to support an application for this course.

TOP TIP

A very important aspect of being an engineer is having a positive 'can do' attitude to life.

Step Four: Use your time wisely

Case study: Getting the balance right

Ali was popular with his colleagues and tutors when he took a BTEC Level 3 Diploma in Aeronautical Engineering. He now works in the advanced materials laboratory of a company that makes lightweight body panels for small, six-seater passenger aircraft.

Ali's job is quite varied and involves discussions with customers, researching the latest developments in hi-tech materials, analysing the results of laboratory tests, and providing technical support to manufacturing engineers.

Since leaving college he has fast-tracked through a graduate apprenticeship and is regarded as something of a 'high flyer' – both in his job and in his hobby of acrobatic flying, which he does at the local airfield. Aviation is his passion.

When studying at college, Ali's main weakness was a lack of self-discipline. This was not deliberate, and was probably caused by his fixation on anything to do with aircraft. He used to go home from college with every intention of working on his assignments but would get side-tracked by reading flying magazines, watching YouTube clips of aeroplanes and running a flight simulator package on his computer.

Ali's tutors were very concerned, as they felt he had great potential which was slipping away. Something needed to be done to get him back on track.

'I didn't realise just how far I was slipping behind – and it was bit of shock realising that I might actually fail the course. The careers adviser was great and arranged two weeks of work experience at the company where I am now employed. I spent time with a project management team and learnt about getting things done on time and to specification. There was a lot happening, but everything was so incredibly well organised that at the end of a hard day's work people still had enough energy to go and enjoy their hobbies. It made me realise that organising your life is really important and that the only person who can do this is yourself.'

Reflection point

Are you able to plan your time effectively, set targets, prioritise tasks and monitor your progress?

Most learners have to combine course commitments with other responsibilities such as a job (either full-time or part-time) and family responsibilities. You will also want to see your friends and keep up your hobbies and interests. Juggling these successfully means you need to be able to use your time wisely.

This involves planning what to do and when to do it to prevent panics about unexpected deadlines. As your course progresses, this becomes even more important as your workload may increase towards the end of a term. In some cases there could be two or more assignments to complete simultaneously. Although tutors try to avoid clashes of this sort, it is sometimes inevitable.

To cope successfully, you need time-management skills, in particular:

- how to organise your time to be more productive
- how to prioritise tasks
- how to overcome time-wasters.

Organising your time

- **Use a diary or wall chart.**
  Using a different colour pen for each, enter:
  - your course commitments, such as assignment dates, tutorials, visits
  - important personal commitments, such as sports matches, family birthdays
  - your work commitments.

TOP TIP

A diary is useful because you can update it as you go, but a wall chart gives you a better overview of your commitments over several weeks. Always keep your diary or chart up to date, and check ahead regularly so that you have prior warning of important dates.

- **Identify how you currently use your time.**
  - Work out how much time you spend at your centre, at work, at home and on social activities.
  - Identify which commitments are vital and which are optional, so you can find extra time if necessary.

- **Plan and schedule future commitments.**
  - Write down any appointments and tasks you must do.
  - Enter assignment review dates and final deadline dates in different colours.
  - This should stop you from arranging a dental appointment on the same morning that you are due to give an important presentation – or planning a hectic social life when you have lots of course work to do.

- **Decide your best times for doing course work.**
  - Expect to do most of your course work in your own time.
  - Work at the time of day when you feel at your best.
  - Work regularly, and in relatively short bursts, rather than once or twice a week for very long stretches.
  - If you're a night owl, allow an hour to 'switch off' before you go to bed.

- **Decide where to work.**
  - Choose somewhere you can concentrate without interruption.
  - Make sure there is space for resources you use, such as books or specialist equipment.
  - You also need good lighting and a good – but not too comfortable – chair.
  - If you can't find suitable space at home, check out your local or college library.

- **Assemble the items you need.**
  - Book ahead to get specific books, journals or DVDs from the library.
  - Ensure you have your notes, handouts and assignment brief with you.
  - Use sticky notes to mark important pages in textbooks or folders.

TOP TIP

Set yourself a target when you start work, so that you feel positive and productive at the end. Always try to end a session when a task is going well, rather than when you are stuck. Then you will be keener to go back to it the next day. Note down outstanding tasks you need to continue with next time.

- **Plan ahead.**
  - If anything is unclear about an assignment, ask your tutor for an explanation as soon as you can.
  - Break down assignments into manageable chunks, such as: find information, decide what to use, create a plan for finished work, write rough draft of first section etc.
  - Work back from deadline dates so that you allow plenty of time to do the work.
  - Always allow more time than you need. It is better to finish early than to run out of time.

TOP TIP

If you are working on a task as a group, organise and agree times to work together. Make sure you have somewhere to meet where you can work without disturbing other courses or groups.

- **Be self-disciplined.**
  - Don't put things off because you're not in the mood. Make it easier by doing simple tasks first to get a sense of achievement. Then move on to something harder.
  - Plan regular breaks. If you're working hard, you need a change of activity to recharge your batteries.
  - If you have a serious problem or personal crisis, talk to your personal tutor promptly.

TOP TIP

Make sure you know the consequences of missing an assignment deadline, as well as the dispensations and exemptions that can be given if you have an unavoidable and serious problem, such as illness (see also page 36).

How to prioritise tasks

Prioritising means doing the most important and urgent task first. Normally this will be the task or assignment with the closest deadline or the one that will most affect your overall course grades.

One way of prioritising is to group tasks into ABC categories.

Category A tasks	These must be done now as they are very important and cannot be delayed, such as completing an assignment to be handed in tomorrow.
Category B tasks	These are jobs you should do if you have time, because otherwise they will rapidly become Category A, such as getting a book that you need for your next assignment.
Category C tasks	These are tasks you should do if you have the time, such as rewriting notes jotted down quickly in a lesson.

Expect to be flexible. For example, if you need to allow time for information to arrive, then send for this first. If you are working in a team, take into account other people's schedules when you are making arrangements.

Avoiding time-wasters

Everyone has days when they don't know where the time has gone. It may be because they were constantly interrupted or because things just kept going wrong. Whatever the reason, the end result is that some jobs don't get done.

If this happens to you regularly, you need to take steps to keep on track. Here are some useful tips.

- **Warn people in advance when you will be working.**
  - Ask them to not interrupt you.
  - If you are in a separate room, shut the door. If someone comes in, make it clear you don't want to talk.
  - If that doesn't work, find somewhere else (or some other time) to work.
- **Switch off your mobile, the television and radio, and your iPod/MP3 player.**
  - Don't respond to, or make, calls or texts.
  - If someone rings your home phone, let voicemail answer or ask them to call back later.
- **Be strict with yourself when you are working online.**
  - Don't check your email until you've finished work.
  - Don't get distracted when searching for information.
  - Keep away from social networking sites.
- **Avoid displacement activities.**
  - These are the normally tedious jobs, such as cleaning your computer screen, that suddenly seem far more attractive than working!

TOP TIP

Benefits to managing your own time include being less stressed (because you are not reacting to problems or crises), producing better work and having time for a social life.

Talking to friends can occupy a lot of time.

TOP TIP

The first step in managing your own time is learning to say 'no' (nicely!) if someone asks you to do something tempting when you should be working.

Key points

- Being in control of your time allows you to balance your commitments according to their importance, and means you won't let anyone down.
- Organising yourself and your time involves knowing how you spend your time now, planning when and where it is best to work, scheduling commitments, and setting sensible timescales to complete your work.
- Knowing how to prioritise means you will schedule work effectively according to its urgency and importance. You will need self-discipline to follow the schedule you have set for yourself.
- Identifying ways in which you may waste time means you can guard against these to achieve your goals more easily.

Action points

1 Start planning your time properly.

a) Find out how many assignments you will have this term, and when you will get them. Put this information into your diary or planner.

b) Update this with your other commitments for the term – both work/course-related and social. Identify possible clashes and decide how to resolve the problem.

c) Identify one major task or assignment you will do soon. Divide it into manageable chunks and decide how long to allow for each chunk, plus some spare time for any problems. If possible, check your ideas with your tutor before you put them into your planner.

2 How good are you at being responsible for your own learning?

a) Fill in this table. Score yourself out of 5 for each area: where 0 is awful and 5 is excellent. Ask a friend or relative to score you as well. See if you can explain any differences.

	Scoring yourself	Other person's score for you
Being punctual		
Organisational ability		
Tidiness		
Working accurately		
Finding and correcting own mistakes		
Solving problems		
Accepting responsibility		
Working with details		
Planning how to do a job		
Using own initiative		
Thinking up new ideas		
Meeting deadlines		

b) Draw up your own action plan for areas where you need to improve. If possible, talk this through at your next **tutorial** (see page 18).

TOP TIP

Don't waste time doing things that distract you when studying for this course. In an engineering business, time costs money.

Activity: Planning and managing resources

Managing a large design project requires detailed planning and management of resources.

For example, think about the new Airbus A380, the so-called superjumbo. Millions of components and sub-assemblies are designed and manufactured in many different countries and then brought together in Toulouse in southern France for final assembly and roll out.

What makes it all happen? What type of person takes responsibility for getting the job done on time? Are you that type of person?

Complete this table.

Type of plan	The information you would need, as a manager, in order to be able to produce the plan
Financial	
Staff recruitment and training	
Design and manufacture of a new product	
Marketing a new product	

Step Five: Utilise all your resources

Case study: Using your resources

Hua studied for a BTEC Level 3 Diploma in Operations and Maintenance Engineering and now works for a company that mass-produces white goods for the domestic market. These include washing machines, tumble dryers and fridges. The company has several hundred employees and has a reputation for selling high-quality products.

The factory operates on a 24/7 basis with a two-week shut down during the end-of-year winter break, which is when major maintenance and replacement of machinery takes place. Throughout the year, scheduled maintenance is carried out by closing down one production line at a time. The factory has a rapid response team of technicians on standby to cope with any unexpected breakdowns and emergencies.

Hua works in the department responsible for planning and scheduling the maintenance operation across the whole factory.

'It's complicated organising the maintenance of machinery that's running for 24 hours a day, because there are so many elements involved. In the maintenance department, we have technicians who are trained for many different types of engineering, including people with specialist knowledge of mechanical, electrical, electronics, robot systems and microprocessors.

'Then you have things like replacement components, consumables, drawings to read, repair procedures, test equipment, and a system for logging when jobs are carried out. We also have to fill out documentation for health and safety reasons, such as the results of portable appliance tests (PAT).

'There are lots of resources that need to be managed and utilised effectively. It's really important to make sure that when a technician starts work on a machine they have everything they need. We can't afford to lose time in our business as it is so competitive.'

Reflection points

Think about the materials and equipment you will need when you start the course. Make a list. For example, have you got the right type of calculator to bring to the first maths class?

Have you got somewhere quiet to work when you are not at college?

Do you know where to get advice if things go wrong?

Your resources are all the things that can help you to be successful in your BTEC Level 3 National qualification, from your favourite website to your **study buddy** (see page 32) who collects handouts for you if you miss a class.

Your centre will provide essential resources, such as a library with appropriate books and electronic reference sources, the computer network, and internet access. You will have to provide basic resources such as pens, pencils and file folders yourself. If you have to buy your own textbooks, look after them carefully so you can sell them on at the end of your course.

Here is a list of resources, with tips for getting the best out of them.

- **Course information**. This includes your course specification, this Study Skills Guide and all information on the Edexcel website relating to your BTEC Level 3 National course. Course information from your centre will include term dates, assignment dates and your timetable. Keep everything safely so you can refer to it whenever you need to clarify something.
- **Course materials**. These include course handouts, printouts, your own notes and textbooks. Put handouts into an A4 folder as soon as you get them. Use a separate folder for each unit you study.

TOP TIP

Filing notes and handouts promptly means they don't get lost, and will stay clean and uncrumpled, and you won't waste time looking for them.

- **Stationery**. You need pens and pencils, a notepad, a hole puncher, a stapler and sets of dividers. Dividers should be clearly labelled to help you store and quickly find notes, printouts and handouts. Your notes should be headed and dated, and those from your own research must also include your source (see Step Eight, page 57 onwards.)
- **People**. Your tutors, specialist staff at college, classmates, your employer and work colleagues, and your relatives and friends are all valuable resources. Many will have particular skills or work in the vocational area that you are studying. Talking to other learners can help to clarify issues that there may not have been time to discuss fully in class.

A **study buddy** is another useful resource as they can make notes and collect handouts if you miss a session. (Remember to return the favour when they are away.)

Always be polite when you are asking people for information. Prepare the questions first and remember that you are asking for help, not trying to get them to do the work for you! If you are interviewing someone for an assignment or project, good preparations are vital. (See Step Eight, page 57 onwards.)

If someone who did the course before you offers help, be careful. It is likely the course requirements will have changed. Never be tempted to copy their assignments (or someone else's). This is **plagiarism** – a deadly sin in the educational world (see also Step Six, page 35.)

TOP TIP

A positive attitude, an enquiring mind and the ability to focus on what is important will have a major impact on your final result.

Key points

- Resources help you to achieve your qualification. Find out what resources you have available to you and use them wisely.
- Have your own stationery items.
- Know how to use central facilities and resources such as the library, learning resource centres and your computer network. Always keep to the policy on IT use in your centre.
- People are a key resource – school or college staff, work colleagues, members of your class, friends, family and people who are experts in their field.

Action points

1 a) List the resources you will need to complete your course successfully. Identify which ones will be provided by your school or college, and which you need to supply yourself.

  b) Go through your list again and identify the resources you already have (or know how to access) and those you don't.

  c) Compare your list with a friend's and decide how to obtain and access the resources you need. Add any items to your list that you forgot.

  d) List the items you still need to get and set a target date for doing this.

2 'Study buddy' schemes operate in many centres. Find out if this applies to your own centre and how you can make the best use of it.

In some you can choose your study buddy, in others people are paired up by their tutor.
- Being a study buddy might mean just collecting handouts when the other person is absent, and giving them important news.

- It may also mean studying together and meeting (or keeping contact by phone or email) to exchange ideas and share resources.

With a study buddy you can share resources and stay on top of the course if you're ever away.

Activity: Using resources

One of the units that you may be studying is Unit 3: Engineering Project. This is a mandatory unit for many BTEC National Engineering qualifications. To achieve the unit you must demonstrate that you can use resources effectively when planning, implementing, monitoring and reviewing your project.

Depending on your interest, choose **one** of the following design briefs:

- Design, construct and test a small practice amplifier for a guitar.
- Design, manufacture and test a clamping device which uses levers and pneumatic cylinders.

Now think about the resources you might need and complete this table.

Resource	Where will you find the resource?	How you will use it?
Background information about the product you are going to make		
Information about the symbols used in electronic/pneumatic circuits		
A CAD package for producing drawings		
Finding out about and obtaining electronic/ pneumatic components and materials		
Health and safety information about soldering components or working with high-pressure fluids		
Test procedures for amplifiers/clamping devices		
Expert help from a third party when sourcing and assembling components		

TOP TIP

Engineering businesses use a range of resources, including money, people, skills, raw materials, tools and machinery when designing and manufacturing products.

Step Six: Understand your assessment

Case study: Gaining the marks you need

Jen is in the second year of a BTEC Level 3 Extended Diploma in Electrical/Electronic Engineering and has been offered a place at university. The entry requirements are high, and she must achieve a final grade of at least DMM.

Her first-year grades showed a steady movement as she gained a greater understanding of how assignments should be tackled, and by the end of the year she had hit her target of achieving merits and distinctions.

This year, however, she is finding some of the units very challenging. She is having to work even harder to achieve her goal, but realises that it will be worth all the effort in the end.

Before starting on an assignment, Jen carefully reads through the brief and plans how she is going to tackle the tasks. She confirms with her tutor that she is on the right track and sets review targets.

'I don't have any real problem with assignments because they always focus on topics that we've been taught in class. The good thing about a BTEC assignment is that you can check

progress with your tutor and, if necessary, improve your grades after it's been marked. This helped a lot in my first year as some of my early assignments were a bit shaky. I only got pass grades. My tutor added feedback and guidance on how to improve my work, and I upped my grades to merit and distinction.

'When you start on a BTEC course it's important to understand that all assignment briefs are laid out in a standard way. To do well, you need to pick up on some of the special terms used in them, particularly command words such as identify, interpret, discuss and analyse.'

Reflection points

When presented with a task, can you plan a solution?

Do you know how to carry out effective research and manage your time?

What is constructive criticism and how can it help you improve your grades?

Why are assignment briefs very rarely 'brief'?

Being successful on any BTEC Level 3 National course means first understanding what you must do in your assignments – and then doing it.

Your assignments focus on topics you have already covered in class. If you've attended regularly, you should be able to complete them confidently.

However, there are some common pitfalls it's worth thinking about. Here are tips to avoid them:

- Read the instructions (the assignment brief) properly and several times before you start.

- Make sure you understand what you are supposed to do. Ask if anything is unclear.

- Complete every part of a task. If you ignore a question, you can't meet the grading criteria.

- Prepare properly. Do your research or reading before you start. Don't guess the answers.

- Communicate your ideas clearly. You can check this by asking someone who doesn't know the subject to look at your work.

- Only include relevant information. Padding out answers makes it look as if you don't know your subject.

- Do the work earlier rather than later to avoid any last-minute panics.

- Pay attention to advice and feedback that your tutor has given you.

The assignment 'brief'

This may be longer than its name implies! The assignment brief includes all the instructions for an assignment and several other details, as you can see in the table below.

What will you find in a BTEC Level 3 National assignment brief?	
Content	**Details**
Title	This will link to the unit and learning outcomes.
Format/style	Written assignment, presentation, demonstration etc.
Preparation	Read case study, do research etc.
Learning outcomes	These state the knowledge you must demonstrate to obtain a required grade.
Grading criterion/ criteria covered	For example, P1, M1, D1.
Individual/group work	Remember to identify your own contribution in any group work.
Feedback	Tutor, peer review.
Interim review dates	Dates to see your tutor.
Final deadline	Last submission date.

Your centre's rules and regulations

Your centre will have several policies and guidelines about assignments, which you need to check carefully. Many, such as those listed below, relate to Edexcel policies and guidelines.

- The procedure to follow if you have a serious problem and can't meet a deadline. An extension may be granted.
- The penalty for missing a deadline without good reason.
- The penalty for copying someone else's work. This is usually severe, so never share your work (or CDs or USB flash drive) with anyone else, and don't borrow theirs.
- **Plagiarism** is also serious misconduct. This means copying someone's work or quoting from books and websites and pretending it is your own work.
- The procedure to follow if you disagree with the grade you are given.

Understanding the question or task

There are two aspects to a question or task. The first is the **command words**, which are described below. The second is the **presentation instructions**, which is what you are asked to do – don't write a report when you should be producing a chart!

Command words, such as 'explain', 'describe', 'analyse', 'evaluate' state how a question must be answered. You may be asked to 'describe' something at pass level, but you will need to do more, perhaps 'analyse' or 'evaluate', to achieve merit or distinction.

Many learners fail to achieve higher grades because they don't realise the difference between these words. Instead of analysing or evaluating they give an explanation instead. Adding more details won't achieve a higher grade – you need to change your whole approach to the answer.

The **grading grid** for each unit of your course gives you the command words, so that you know what to do to achieve a pass, merit or distinction. The tables that follow show you what is usually required when you see a particular command word. These are just examples to guide you, as the exact response will depend on the question. If you have any doubts, check with your tutor before you start work.

There are two important points to note.

- A command word such as 'create' or 'explain' may be repeated in the grading criteria for different grades. In these cases the complexity or range of the task itself increases at the higher grades.
- Command words vary depending on your vocational area. So Art and Design grading

grids may use different command words from Applied Science, for example.

TOP TIP

Look at this section again when you get your first assignment and check the command words against these explanations.

To obtain a pass grade

To achieve a pass you must usually demonstrate that you understand the important facts relating to a topic and can state these clearly and concisely.

Command words for a pass	Meaning
Create (or produce)	Make, invent or construct an item.
Describe	Give a clear, straightforward description that includes all the main points and links these together logically.
Define	Clearly explain what a particular term means and give an example, if appropriate, to show what you mean.
Explain … how/why	Set out in detail the meaning of something, with reasons. It is often helpful to give an example of what you mean. Start with the topic then give the 'how' or 'why'.
Identify	Distinguish and state the main features or basic facts relating to a topic.
Interpret	Define or explain the meaning of something.
Illustrate	Give examples to show what you mean.
List	Provide the information required in a list rather than in continuous writing.
Outline	Write a clear description that includes all the main points but avoid going into too much detail.
Plan (or devise)	Work out and explain how you would carry out a task or activity.
Select (and present) information	Identify relevant information to support the argument you are making and communicate this in an appropriate way.
State	Write a clear and full account.
Undertake	Carry out a specific activity.
Examples:	
Identify the main features on a digital camera.	
Outline the steps to take to carry out research for an assignment.	

To obtain a merit grade

To obtain a merit you must prove that you can apply your knowledge in a specific way.

Command words for a merit	Meaning
Analyse	Identify separate factors, say how they relate to each other and how each one relates to the topic.
Classify	Sort your information into appropriate categories before presenting or explaining it.
Compare and contrast	Identify the main factors that apply in two or more situations and explain the similarities and differences or advantages and disadvantages.
Demonstrate	Provide several relevant examples or appropriate evidence which support the arguments you are making. In some vocational areas this may also mean giving a practical performance.
Discuss	Provide a thoughtful and logical argument to support the case you are making.
Explain (in detail)	Provide details and give reasons and/or evidence to clearly support the argument you are making.
Implement	Put into practice or operation. You may also have to interpret or justify the effect or result.
Interpret	Understand and explain an effect or result.
Justify	Give appropriate reasons to support your opinion or views and show how you arrived at these conclusions.
Relate/report	Give a full account, with reasons.
Research	Carry out a full investigation.
Specify	Provide full details and descriptions of selected items or activities.
Examples: Compare and contrast the performance of two different digital cameras. Explain in detail the steps to take to research an assignment.	

To obtain a distinction grade

To obtain a distinction you must prove that you can make a reasoned judgement based on appropriate evidence.

Command words for a distinction	Meaning
Analyse	Identify the key factors, show how they are linked and explain the importance and relevance of each.
Assess	Give careful consideration to all the factors or events that apply, and identify which are the most important and relevant, with reasons.
Comprehensively explain	Give a very detailed explanation that covers all the relevant points, and give reasons for your views or actions.
Critically comment	Give your view after you have considered all the evidence, particularly the importance of both the relevant positive and negative aspects.
Evaluate	Review the information and then bring it together to form a conclusion. Give evidence to support each of your views or statements.
Evaluate critically	Review the information to decide the degree to which something is true, important or valuable. Then assess possible alternatives, taking into account their strengths and weaknesses if they were applied instead. Then give a precise and detailed account to explain your opinion.
Summarise	Identify/review the main, relevant factors and/or arguments so that these are explained in a clear and concise manner.
Examples:	
Assess ten features commonly found on a digital camera.	
Analyse your own ability to carry out effective research for an assignment.	

TOP TIP

Check that you understand exactly how you need to demonstrate each of the learning outcomes specified in the assignment.

Responding positively

Assignments enable you to demonstrate what you know and how you can apply it. You should respond positively to the challenge and give it your best shot. Being well organised and having confidence in your own abilities helps too, and this is covered in the next section.

Key points

- Read instructions carefully so that you don't make mistakes that can easily be avoided, such as only doing part of the set task.

- Note the assignment deadline on your planner and any interim review dates. Schedule work around these dates to make the most of reviews with your tutor.

- Check your centre's policies relating to assignments, such as how to obtain an extension or query a final grade.

- Expect command words and/or the complexity of a task to be different at higher grades, because you have to demonstrate higher-level skills.

TOP TIP

All your assignments will relate to topics you have covered and work you have done in class. They're not meant to be a test to catch you out.

Action points

1 Check your ability to differentiate between different types of command words by doing this activity.
   a) Prepare a brief description of your usual lifestyle (pass level).
   b) Describe and justify your current lifestyle (merit level).
   c) Critically evaluate your current lifestyle (distinction level).

It would be a good idea to check that your answer is accurate and appropriate by showing it to your tutor at your next tutorial.

TOP TIP

When presenting evidence for an assessment, think about the person who will be looking through it. Plan your 'pitch' well and make it easy for the assessor to match your evidence against the grading criteria.

Sample assignment

Note about assignments
All learners are different and will approach their assignments in different ways.
The sample assignment that follows shows how one learner answered a brief to achieve pass, merit and distinction level criteria. This learner work shows just one way in which these grading criteria can be evidenced. There are no standard or set answers. If you produce the required evidence for each task, then you will achieve the grading criteria covered by the assignment.

Front sheet

When putting evidence together, check that it meets the requirements of the grading criterion.

Make sure that you know about your centre's policy on meeting deadlines.

Before submitting your work it is useful to run it past your tutor for comment. There may be essential evidence that you have missed.

Check that for a particular criterion your evidence adequately covers the topics that are in the unit content range statement.

Learner name		Assessor name	
David Webber		Tracey Thomson	
Date issued	**Completion date**		**Submitted on**
12 October 2010	15 November 2010		15 November 2010
Qualification		**Unit**	
BTEC Level 3 National Engineering		Unit 1 Health and Safety in the Engineering Workplace	

Assignment title	Controlling hazards and risks in the workplace

In this assessment you will have opportunities to provide evidence against the following criteria.
Indicate the page numbers where the evidence can be found.

Criteria reference	To achieve the criteria the evidence must show that the student is able to:	Task no.	Page numbers
P3	describe the methods used to identify hazards in a working environment	1	1
P4	describe how hazards which become risks can be controlled	2a, b	2
P5	carry out a risk assessment on a typical item/area of the working environment	3a	3–5
P6	suggest suitable control measures after a risk assessment has been carried out and state the reasons why they are suitable	3c	3–5
M2	explain the importance of carrying out all parts of a risk assessment in a suitable manner	3b	3–5
M3	explain how control measures are used to prevent accidents	4	6
D1	justify the methods used to deal with hazards in accordance with workplace policies and legal requirements	5	7

Learner declaration

I certify that the work submitted for this assignment is my own and research sources are fully acknowledged.

Learner signature: *David Webber*   Date: *12 October 2010*

Make sure that any evidence you present is your own and not copied or cut and pasted from other people's work.

Acknowledge any reference sources at the end of your portfolio.

Assignment brief

Unit title	Unit 1: Health and Safety in the Engineering Workplace
Qualification	BTEC Level 3 National Diploma in Engineering
Start date	12 October 2010
Deadline date	15 November 2010
Assessor	Tracey Thomson

Assignment title	Controlling hazards and risks in the workplace

The purpose of this assignment is to provide a framework where the learner:
- knows how to identify and control hazards in the workplace
- is able to carry out a risk assessment and identify control measures.

Scenario
You work as a metal fitter for a small general engineering company and you have been tasked with carrying out a risk assessment of your metal working machine shop. The shop has:
- four lathes;
- an electrically powered guillotine;
- an electrically powered pillar drill; and
- an abrasive wheel grinding machine (used for sharpening tools).

There is also a storage area and racking for metal bar and sheet metal; the metal bar is used for lathe work and the large sections of sheet metal have to be guillotined to provide suitably sized work pieces.

The shop is equipped with appropriate first aid and fire points. Adjacent to the machine shop there is a physically separate tool store, restroom, washroom and toilets. These are not considered part of the machine shop and do not need to be risk assessed at this time.

There is a total of one new fitter, four experienced fitters (including yourself) and one supervisor who work regularly in and around the machine shop.

Scenarios are intended to help you relate the assignment tasks to the real world of engineering.

Competence in carrying out a practical task should be confirmed by a tutor-signed witness statement.

Task 1
Describe the methods/procedure you will adopt to identify the hazards in your metal working machine shop.

This provides evidence for P3

Task 2
Define 'hazard' and 'risk' in terms of health and safety.
Identify the hazards for any one piece of machinery in your metal working shop and for those hazards that offer most risk, describe how they are controlled.

This provides evidence for P4

Task 3
Using the five-step method, carry out a risk assessment for all machinery and areas of your metalwork machine shop, recording your findings in a suitable manner, using a standardised form of risk assessment paperwork. (P5)

Explain the importance of carrying out all parts of your workshop risk assessment in a suitable standardised manner, including the implications for not following a suitable procedure. (M2)

After carrying out your risk assessment, suggest suitable control measures for the workshop area as a whole, giving reasons as to their suitability. (P6)

This provides evidence for P5, P6 and M2

Task 4
Explain in general terms how control measures are used to prevent accidents.

This provides evidence for M3

Task 5
Justify, in writing, the methods used to deal with the hazards in your metalwork shop, in accordance with local policies and legal requirements.

This provides evidence for D1

Sources of information
HSE, *Essentials of health and safety at work* Fourth edition 2006 – ISBN 0717661792
http://www.hse.gov.uk

This brief has beeen verified as being fit for purpose			
Assessor	Tracey Thomson		
Signature	Tracey Thomson	Date	1 October 2010
Internal verifier	Fred Brown		
Signature	Fred Brown	Date	1 October 2010

When searching for information in complex resources such as the HSE website, you can save time by asking your tutor for guidance.

Sample learner work

Starting with the HSE as a reference and presenting a checklist is good practice because it focuses your efforts.

Sample learner work: page 1

Health and Safety in the Engineering Workplace

Task 1 (P3)
Describe the methods/procedure you will adopt to identify the hazards in your metal working machine shop.

In order to identify hazards I will first consult the HSE guidance "Five steps to risk assessment" (http://www.hse.gov.uk/risk/fivesteps.htm). Also I will consult the guidance provided in the HSE information leaflet: *using work equipment safely* (INDG 229), where I happen to know there is some good H&S information on engineering machines.

Then following HSE guidance, I will:
• walk around all the areas in the workshop where the fitters work and where visitors walk, noting things that might pose a risk, taking into account the above guidance and the guidance given in the HSE book, *Essentials of health and safety at work*
• talk with our H&S representative and shop supervisor concerning any particular problems/hazards they may be aware of, that might pose a risk
• look at our accident book, to see the problems we have had in the past
• write down on our risk assessment form, the people that could be harmed by the hazards and how they might be harmed
• write down on the same form, what is being done to control the hazards and my suggestions where the control measures seemed to be inadequate to meet H&S requirements
• discuss my findings with our supervisor and H&S representative, then after considering their advice and using their help, I would put my findings into practice.

A good choice of machine because it presents a number of hazards.

Simple one-line answers are perfectly acceptable because the task starts with the word 'define'. If it had said 'describe', then each answer would be three or four lines long.

Sample learner work: page 2

Task 2 (P4)

a) Define "hazard" and "risk" in terms of health and safety.

A *hazard* is anything that might cause harm, such as working on ladders, spilt liquids or machine cutting tools. *Risk* is the chance of harm being done, as well as how serious that harm could be.

b) Identify the hazards for any one piece of machinery in your metal working shop and for those hazards that offer most risk, describe how they are controlled.

Centre Lathe hazards: The centre lathe has moving parts and uses sharp cutting tools so hazards are:
1) possible entanglement of hair, loose clothing, dangling jewellery etc
2) crush injuries from moving work piece or platform
3) people can be struck by moving parts or ejected material
4) cuts and severing injuries due to cutting tools and ejected swarf
5) shock hazard from electrical supply.

1) Ensure protective cap is used to keep back hair, ensure no dangling jewellery is worn, rings etc. are taped up or removed, protective clothing is buttoned up, pockets are zipped up and no loose objects protrude.
2) Centre lathe is guarded from dangerous moving parts and warning notices posted.
3) Ejected material and moving parts are guided away or shielded from walkways and the machine operator.
4) Suitable guarding and warning notices (placed on or near the machine).
5) Motor cabling should be shielded, a supply circuit breaker should be provided at the power distribution point and a power emergency trip switch should be attached to the lathe body and clearly marked.

This answer is a simple statement, not an explanation as asked for in the grading criterion. People will always have accidents – you should be explaining how to manage the consequences of an accident and reduce its severity. You also need to explain the legal implications of not following recommended procedures, and the involvement of the HSE if an accident does occur.

Sample learner work: page 3

Task 3 (P5, P6 and M2)

a) Using the five-step method, carry out a risk assessment for all machinery and areas of your metalwork machine shop, recording your findings in a suitable manner, using a standardised form of risk assessment paperwork. (P5)

Please see risk assessment report form attached.

b) Explain the importance of carrying out all parts of your workshop risk assessment in a suitable standardised manner, including the implications for not following a suitable procedure. (M2)

It is important to carry out a risk assessment properly so that nothing gets forgotten and people do not have accidents.

c) After carrying out your risk assessment, suggest suitable control measures for the workshop area as a whole, giving reasons as to their suitability. (P6)

Please see risk assessment report form attached.

Get someone to take a photograph of you carrying out the risk assessment and also ask your tutor for a signed witness statement confirming that you performed to a satisfactory standard.

Sample learner work: page 4

Risk assessment report form

What are the hazards?	Who might be harmed and how?	What are we already doing? (Control measures)
Machinery (Lathes Pillar drill Abrasive wheel Grinding machine Guillotine)	Fitters and others may suffer serious injury from unguarded moving parts of machinery	• All dangerous parts of all machines guarded to manufacturers standards • Machinery guards checked monthly and maintained in good condition • All experienced fitters trained and certified as competent to work on lathes, pillar drill, abrasive grinder and guillotine • All workshop personnel are required to wear safety shoes, protective clothing and eye protection when operating machines • Warning and operating notices posted at machines • All machines fitted with electrical isolation and emergency stop switches • Supervisor trained and experienced with all machines, ensures that all fitters carry out pre-use daily checks, prior to operating machines
Manual handling	Fitters and others may suffer back injury and cut injuries when handling bar stock and large sheets of metal	• All fitters trained in manual handling • Suitable gauntlets and other lifting aids placed in prominent position
Electricity	Fitters/maintainers/ contractors may suffer shock and burn injuries from faulty electrical supplies to machines and building electrical installations	• Maintainers and contractors and relevant others discuss electrical safety before each job begins to ensure that relevant machinery, circuits etc are isolated and locked-off, during job • Electrical installation and all electrical supplies to machines is inspected and maintained to a planned schedule
Workshop General Slips and trips	Fitters, contractors and visitors may suffer injuries if they slip on spillages, or trip over objects and fall	• Procedures for good housekeeping adhered to (eg procedures for oil and coolant spillages etc) • Floors generally in good condition • Walkways clearly marked • Good lighting throughout
Fire	Any staff, contractors, visitors trapped in workshop could suffer fatal injury from smoke inhalation or burns	• Fire risk assessment done as at www.fire.gov. uk/workplace+safety and necessary action • All contracting staff and other visiting workers, told of fire and evacuation policy, before work begins
Working at height	Maintenance staff and/ or contractors may suffer severe injury, if they fall from height (eg when changing light filaments or refurbishing building/ fittings)	• All maintenance and contracting jobs involved with working at height, discussed with supervisor and other relevant staff and a safe system of work agreed before job begins • Access equipment (eg ladders, tower scaffold) kept in workshop, checked before use and stored safely after use

This tabular method is good because it follows standard industry practice.

This is a proper explanation because it contains your thoughts about control methods.

Task 4 (M3)

Explain in general terms how control measures are used to prevent accidents.

Control measures in general are designed to consider all workplace hazards and put in place not only immediate actions, but also policies and procedures that reduce or if possible eliminate the risk associated with these hazards developing into safety incidents or accidents.

It is therefore not good enough, for example, just to post a notice warning operators of the need to wear safety glasses when using a grinding machine. There also need to be control measures that provide operator training and general safety awareness, as well as a means of checking that the immediate safety control measures at the machine are complied with.

In my own workshop it can be seen from my risk assessment report that eliminating or minimising the risk at the workface depends on other control measures that have often been introduced remote from the machine or hazard. An example is the control measures introduced for electrical hazards, whereby the building electrical installation and electrical wiring to the machines not only comply with the wiring regulations and have the appropriate circuit isolation devices and warning notices but are also subject to regular inspection, as part of a planned schedule.

Thus the control measures policy and procedures ensure that there is a chain or series of control measures in place, so that if one gets overlooked, although risk may be increased, providing the other control measures in the series are adhered to, an accident or serious incident is unlikely.

Putting the hazards into groups is a good idea because it allows you to be focused when justifying a particular control strategy.

Making reference to relevant legislation adds weight to the answers.

Task 5 (D1)

Justify, in writing, the methods used to deal with the hazards in your metalwork shop, in accordance with local policies and legal requirements.

With reference to my risk assessment report I have divided the identified hazards into four areas: machinery, manual handling, electricity and the workshop in general. Under each of these hazard headings, I have given reasons from both a technical and legislative perspective, in an attempt to justify the use of these methods, in our workshop.

Machinery
- Guards
- Checks
- Jigs
- Fixtures
- Eye protection
- Training
- Maintenance
- Protective clothing

To ensure safe operation of machines, protection of fitters and others against the ejection of swarf, sparks from grinding machine, movement of work piece and machine parts and entrapment of loose clothing. The use of these methods also ensures that employers and employees follow best safe practice, execute their responsibilities and comply with HSE guidance and H&S legislation, including the Health and Safety at Work Act 1974, Personal Protective Equipment Regulation 1992, Management of Health and Safety at Work Regulations 1999, Provision and Use of Work Equipment Regulations (PUWER) 1998.

Manual handling
Use of:
- lifting aids
- gloves
- safety footwear
- other protective clothing
- warning notices

To help prevent lift injuries and cuts from the sheet metal edges and to ensure safe feed of sheet metal through guillotine. The use of these methods also ensures that employees and employers execute their responsibilities and comply with the H&S legislation listed above (under machinery). In addition these control methods also ensure that the company and individuals comply with the Manual Handling Operations Regulations 1992, as well as following best practice as laid down in HSE guidance pamphlets.

Electricity
- Isolation switches
- Emergency stop switches
- Circuit breakers
- Isolation procedures
- Regular inspection of electrical installations
- Cabling, shrouds and machine connections/fittings

To help prevent injuries resulting from electric shock and electrical equipment burns. In addition these control methods also ensure that employees and employers execute their responsibilities and comply with the H&S legislation listed above (under machinery), as well as ensuring compliance with the Electricity at Work Regulations 1998.

The blocks of text contain sentences that are more than just simple statements and so meet the D1 criterion of being justifications.

Assessor's comments

There will be assignments where you have to search for information that may be difficult to find. Before starting work ask a tutor or someone with specialist knowledge for guidance.

The learner may want to think about improving his evidence for this criterion.

For any assignment always check that you are achieving the pass (P) criteria. To achieve an overall pass for a unit you must get all the Ps signed off. Miss out on just one of them, and the unit could be lost.

Qualification	BTEC Level 3 National Diploma in Engineering	Year	2010–2011
Unit number and title	Unit 1: Health and Safety in the Engineering Workplace	Learner name	David Webber

Grading criteria	Achieved?
P3 Describe the methods used to identify hazards in a working environment	Y
P4 Describe how hazards which become risks can be controlled	Y
P5 Carry out a risk assessment on a typical item/area of the working environment	Y
P6 Suggest suitable control measures after a risk assessment has been carried out and state the reasons why they are suitable	Y
M2 Explain the importance of carrying out all parts of a risk assessment in a suitable manner	N
M3 Explain how control measures are used to control accidents	Y
D1 Justify the methods used to deal with hazards in accordance with workplace policies and legal requirements	Y

Learner feedback

It was difficult to find outside information for the risk assessment.

Assessor feedback

You have given clear, comprehensive and relevant answers to tasks 1 and 2 that meet the criteria P3 and P4 in full.

Your risk assessment report has been logically presented and you have clearly followed the HSE guidance as to how a risk assessment should be carried out and reported on. You have included a range of control measures in your report and have therefore achieved criteria P5 and P6. My only comment is that you did not mention specifically anything on your workshops control measures for first aid, such as the keeping of an up-to-date accident book, eye wash facilities and a list of qualified/duty first aid personnel. However, that aside, all other areas of H&S were covered.

Your answer to task 3b was very brief and rather disappointing, when compared with all other aspects of your work. It is a shame that you did not approach me for guidance on this task before submitting your assignment if you were having difficulties. What you have submitted in answer to this task unfortunately does not meet the criteria for achievement of M2. There will be an opportunity for you to meet M2, when you are given assignment 3. In the meantime you would be wise to research the importance of carrying out a risk assessment. I will speak to you in class about this topic when you receive this feedback.

Your answers to tasks 4 and 5 are excellent, and your depth of understanding on control methods and the justification for your company policies and procedures for such methods is outstanding and clearly meets the criteria for M3 and D1. Well done!

Action plan

Assessor signature	Tracey Thomson		Date	20 Nov 2010
Learner signature	David Webber		Date	20 Nov 2010

Detailing what you enjoyed and also any problems that you had will help you in future assignments. It may also help your tutor when they come to revise the assignment. They may decide to put in more information about links to resources.

If your tutor makes positive criticism when things are wrong and provides guidance on how to put them right, this is all part of the leaning process. Always think about how to improve any aspect of your work that is not up to scratch; action planning is a good way to do this.

The assessor has given good feedback. David should accept her praise and pick up on areas of concern.

Step Seven: Work productively as a member of a group

Case study: Workplace teams

Joel recently started work as an apprentice with a business that designs, manufactures and installs packaging machines. Ppack Ltd employs about 100 people and has contracts with businesses that supply processed food to the major supermarkets.

The company has enrolled Joel at the local further education college on a BTEC Level 3 Diploma in Mechanical Engineering. He has the correct number of GCSEs for direct entry onto the course.

Ppack has a flat management structure and is split into four divisions:

- Design and development
- Manufacture
- Installation and commissioning
- Sales and customer services.

The company was set up ten years ago by two young engineers, Trish and Dave, who'd met while studying on National and Higher National engineering programmes. Trish and Dave have worked very hard to grow the business. Over the years they've built up a very loyal team of workers who are keen to see the business grow even further. All employees are signed up to a company share purchase scheme, which is linked to company profits.

Joel first met Trish and Dave when they visited his school to talk about careers in engineering and to explain how they started the business from a small unit on the local business park.

'What surprised me about Dave and Trish is their management style. I'd always imagined that company directors would be a bit intimidating, and would want to get their own way all the time. Workers would be told what to do and managers would push them to work even harder.

'What I discovered from that meeting, and also since starting work, is that it's different at Ppack. Everyone works as a team player, and the managers ensure that people's strengths are put to best use. Workers have different skill levels and abilities, but all are treated equally and their contribution to the success of the business valued. In each division there are teams; each has a team leader who reports back to the directors.

'I'm a first-year apprentice but I have already sat in on a couple of team meetings – at one of them, I was asked to check through some calculations as they know I got an A* for my GCSE maths, and that I'm good with figures. Later in the day I bumped into Dave and he said how pleased they are with my progress to date – I went home feeling great.'

Reflection points

Think about team situations you have been in. Do you usually speak out more than you observe and listen? Or vice versa?

Think about why a team needs a leader. How would you choose a team leader?

In your private life, you can choose your own friends, whereas at work you are paid to work alongside many people, whether you like them or not. This applies at school or college too. Hopefully, by now, you've outgrown wanting to only work with your best friends on every project.

You may not be keen on everyone in your team, but you should still be pleasant and cooperative. This may be harder if you are working with a partner than in a large group.

Sometimes you may be the group leader. This may inspire you, or fill you with dread. You won't be expected to develop team-leader skills overnight, but it helps if you know the basics.

First, you should understand how groups and teams work and why good teamwork is considered vital by employers.

Working in groups and teams

If you have a full-time or part-time job, you already belong to a working group or team. At school or college your class is an example of a working group.

All working groups have some common characteristics:

- doing the same type of work – though in the workplace you probably have different roles or responsibilities
- a group leader or supervisor
- a reason for working together, such as studying for the same qualification or tackling an area of work too large for someone to do alone
- group members are dependent on each other in some way; at work you may have to cover someone's workload if they are absent
- group members concentrate on their individual achievements and success.

A team is different. As a team member you have a specific objective to achieve **together** – and this is more important than the goals of individual team members.

> **TOP TIP**
>
> Understanding how groups and teams function will help you be a better team worker and a better team leader.

These are the characteristics of a team:

- Team members have a team goal which is more important than any personal goals.
- Team members have complementary skills so that the team can achieve more than individuals working alone could achieve.
- Work is allocated to play to each person's strengths and talents.
- The team members give each other encouragement and support.
- There is collective responsibility for achieving the goal.

A good team leader acts as facilitator and motivator, and gives practical support and guidance.

Working in a team has many benefits. Team members can learn from each other and combine their skills to do a better job more quickly. Working with other people is often more enjoyable than working alone, too. Many industries rely heavily on efficient group working, from IT teams to health workers and the emergency services.

> **TOP TIP**
>
> Focusing on the task rather than on personalities is the first step in learning to work with different people whose views may not match your own.

There are many benefits to be gained from working as a team.

Being a good team member

Everyone wants team members who are talented, positive, cheerful and full of energy. These are the key areas to focus on if you wish to be a good team member.

- **Your social skills.** This includes being courteous, treating other people as you wish to be treated, saying 'please' when you want something and thanking people who do you a favour.

- **Your temperament**. Expect people to have different views and opinions from you, and don't take offence if someone disagrees with you. If you lose your temper easily, learn to walk away before you say something you may regret.

- **Your communication skills.** This includes talking and listening!

Practise saying what you mean clearly, accurately and succinctly. Be prepared to give good reasons to justify your arguments and ideas.

Allow people to finish what they're saying, without interruption, before you talk. Never shout people down. Think before you speak so that you don't upset people with tactless remarks. If you inadvertently do so, apologise.

- **Your commitment.** Always keep your promises and never let anyone down when they are depending upon you. Always do your fair share of the work, even if you don't agree with all the decisions made by your team. Tell people promptly if you are having problems so there is time to solve them. Be loyal to your team when you're talking to other people.

Being the team leader

It can be difficult to strike a balance between 'leading' the team and working with friends. You need to inspire and motivate your team without being bossy or critical.

Important points to remember about being a team leader

- Lead by example. Stay pleasant, consistent and control your temper, even under pressure.
- Everyone is different. Your ways of working may not always be the best.
- Be prepared to listen and contribute positively to a discussion.
- Encourage quieter team members to join in discussions by asking for their views.
- Be prepared to do whatever you ask other people to do.
- Note down what you say you will do, so that you don't forget.
- Discuss alternatives with people rather than giving orders.
- Be sensitive to other people's feelings. They may have personal problems or issues that affect their behaviour.
- Learn the art of persuasion.
- Act as peacemaker. Help people reach a compromise when necessary.
- Give team members the credit for their hard work or good ideas.
- Admit your mistakes. Look for a positive solution and think about what can be learned for the future, rather than making excuses.
- Praise and encourage team members who are working hard.
- Make criticisms constructively, and in private.
- Be assertive (put forward your point of view firmly) rather than aggressive (attacking other people to defend yourself).

Some notes of caution about being a team leader

- Try to look pleasant and don't glare at people who interrupt you unexpectedly.
- Never talk about team members behind their backs.
- Don't gossip, exaggerate to make a point, spread rumours, speculate or tell lies.
- Don't expect to get your own way all the time – all good leaders back down on occasion.
- Never criticise any colleagues in front of other people. Speak to them in private and keep it constructive.

TOP TIP

Excellent ideas often come from quiet team members. Encourage everyone to make suggestions so that you don't overlook any valuable contributions.

Key points

- There are many benefits of working in a group or as a team. These include mutual support, companionship and the exchange of ideas.
- You will be expected to work cooperatively with other people at work, and during many course assignments.

- It isn't easy learning to be a team leader. Team leaders should be fair, consistent and pleasant to work with, as well as loyal and sensitive to the needs of team members.

Action points

1 Identify the role of teamwork in your area of study. Identify the team's goal and any factors you think will contribute towards its success.

2 Decide how you would handle each of the following difficult situations if you were the team leader. If you can, discuss your ideas with a friend in your class.
   a) The team needs to borrow a college video camera to record an event being held tonight. Your tutor tells you that the one you reserved last week is not working and the rest are out on loan.
   b) A member of your team has personal problems so you have given him less work to do. Now you've been accused of having favourites.
   c) A team member is constantly letting everyone down because of poor work and non-attendance at group meetings.
   d) Two team members have disagreed about how to do a task. You're not bothered how they do it as long as it gets done properly, and by the deadline.
   e) A team member becomes very aggressive whenever she is challenged in any way – no matter how mildly.

3 Identify someone who has inspired you because they've been an excellent leader. This could be someone you've met, a fictional character or a famous person. Note down what it is about them that impressed you.

TOP TIP

Team working, and bouncing ideas around, produces quicker and better results than working in isolation. Engineering businesses actively encourage team working.

Activity: Individual team member's skills

The technical director of an engineering business has set up a team meeting to carry out a new product design review. Each member of the team has specific skills that will be needed – can you identify at least one of them for each team member? Make a note of these skills in the table on the next page

Team member	Skills
Technical director co-ordinates design process Final desision of Product.	They have a very specific set of supervision skills across every position in the company. They line manage chief designers
Chief designer co-ordinating all design activities.	The chief designer is assigned to a depart -ment and directly reports to the technical director. There is line mangement to the senior designer
Senior designer Physically does design work	The job description is a person in a position indipendantly required to direct a small design factor in a company. They are very hands on.
CAD draftsperson specific proffession	The main design criteria is run and imagined into a CAD itteration. They convert production drawings into a sample cad model.
Manufacturing engineer specification	The manufacturing engineers are in charge of the application to build the final product and proto types. Technical assistant to finish the specification.
CNC machine tool technician specification	They will setup, edit and control the machinery and electronic devices in the company
Marketing manager	They find a niche market and create exposure for the companies products.
Company accountant	Analyzing data to managing finances and budgets to ensure compliance

Step Eight: Understand how to research and analyse information

Case study: Finding and analysing information about jobs

The second year of the BTEC Level 3 Extended Diploma in Manufacturing Engineering is going well for Becky and she is fired up about the next stage of her career. Becky has decided to take up an apprenticeship and to continue with her studies at college. She has been for several interviews and has been offered positions by two local businesses.

One company is a small family-run concern that makes sheet metal products such as ducting for air conditioning systems, racking systems and storage hoppers for grain. Most of its products are made to special order, and a designer usually visits the customer to agree a specification. A drawing is produced on a CAD system, and manufacture is carried out by a small team. The finished product is fitted by the company's own installation technicians.

The second company is a large multinational that has a manufacturing facility in Becky's home town. It produces large quantities of very high-quality fluid control equipment that is fitted to oil rigs, chemical distillation plants and pharmaceutical manufacturing machinery. The company uses a flexible manufacturing system (FMS) and can turn around a new design in less than 24 hours. Products are boxed and put on pallets for distribution to the customer. The business is very 'hi-tech', and the company keeps staff up to date with latest developments by running in-house training sessions.

Becky has a difficult decision to make. 'I find the manufacturing side of engineering really interesting. The vacuum-forming machine we had at school was great, particularly when we worked in a team to produce a batch of components that were all the same. The problem I have is deciding which apprenticeship offer to accept.

'I know quite a lot about the small company, but less about the large one – it's using a manufacturing system that I'm not familiar with and I don't know much about chemicals and pharmaceuticals. I need to do some research!'

Reflection points

Think about how you research information. Are your current techniques effective?

Where would you start if you wanted to find information about a company?

How would you find out about a new manufacturing product?

As a BTEC Level 3 National learner, you often have to find information for yourself. This skill will be invaluable in your working life and if you continue your studies at higher education level. Sometimes the information will give you a better understanding of a topic, at other times you will research information for a project or assignment. Sometimes you may be so interested in something that you want to find out more without being told to do so!

Whatever your reason, and no matter where your information can be found, there is a good and not-so-good way to go about the task. This section will help if you can't find what you want, or find too much, or drift aimlessly around a library, or watch a demonstration and don't know what to ask afterwards.

Types of information

There are many types of information and many different sources. Depending on the task, these are the sources you may need to consult.

- **Verbal information.** This includes talking to friends, colleagues at work, members of your family, listening to experts explain what they do, interviewing people, talking to sales reps at an exhibition or customers about a product.

- **Printed information**. This includes information printed in newspapers, journals, magazines, books, posters, workshop manuals, leaflets and catalogues. The type of magazine or newspaper you read may have its own slant on the information, which you may have to take into account (see page 67).

- **Written information**. This includes course notes and handouts, reports and other documents in the workplace. If you want to use written information from work, you must check this is allowed, and that it doesn't contain confidential material such as financial information or staff names and addresses.

- **Graphical information.** This includes illustrations, pictures, cartoons, line drawings, graphs and photographs. Graphics can make something clearer than words alone. For example, a satnav instruction book might contain illustrations to show different procedures.

- **Electronic information.** This includes information from electronic sources such as DVDs, CD-ROMs, searchable databases, websites, podcasts, webinars (**seminars** online), emails and text messages. The huge amount of information available online is both a help and a hindrance. You can find information quickly, but the source may be unreliable, out of date, inaccurate or inappropriate (see page 60.)

TOP TIP

Too much information is as bad as too little, because it's overwhelming. The trick is to find good quality, relevant information and know when to call a halt to your search.

TOP TIP

Consider all appropriate sources and don't just rely on information found online.

Finding what you need

Spend a few minutes planning what to do before you start looking for information. This can save a lot of time later on.

The following steps will help you to do this.

1 Make sure you understand exactly what it is you need to know so that you don't waste time looking for the wrong thing.

2 Clarify your objectives to narrow down your search. Think about why the information is wanted and how much detail you need. For example, learners studying BTEC Nationals in Engineering and Performing Arts may both be researching 'noise' for their projects but they are likely to need different types of information and use it in different ways.

3 Identify your sources and check you know how to use them. You need to choose sources that are most likely to provide information relevant to your objectives. For example, an engineering learner might find information on noise emissions in industry journals and by checking out specialist websites.

4 Plan and schedule your research. Theoretically, you could research information for ever. Knowing when to call a halt takes skill. Write a schedule that states when you must stop looking and start sorting the information.

5 Store your information safely in a labelled folder. This folder should include printouts or photocopies of articles, notes about events you have attended or observed, photographs you've taken or sketches you've drawn. Divide your information under topic headings to make it easier to find. When you're ready to start work, re-read your assignment brief and select the items that are most closely related to the task you are doing.

TOP TIP

Allocate time for research as part of your assignment task. Take into account any interim deadlines as well as the final deadline for completing the work.

Primary and secondary research, and the law of copyright

There are two ways to research information. One is known as primary research, the other is secondary research.

Primary research

Primary research involves finding new information about an issue or topic. This might include finding out people's views about a product or interviewing an expert. When carrying out interviews, you will need to design a survey or questionnaire. Your primary research might also include observing or experiencing something for yourself, and recording your feelings and observations.

Secondary research

Secondary research involves accessing information that already exists in books, files, newspapers or on CD-ROMs, computer databases or the internet, and assessing it against your objectives.

This information has been prepared by other people and is available to anyone. You can quote from an original work provided you acknowledge the source of your information. You should put this acknowledgement in your text or in the bibliography to your text; do not claim it as your own research. You must include the author's name, year of publication, the title and publisher, or the web address if it is an online article. You should practise listing the sources of articles so

that you feel confident writing a bibliography. Use the guidance sheet issued by your centre to help you. This will illustrate the style your centre recommends. (See also page 62.)

The trick with research is to choose the best technique to achieve your objectives, and this may mean using a mix of methods and resources. For example, if you have to comment on an industry event you might go to it, make notes, interview people attending, observe the event (perhaps take a video camera), and read any newspaper reports or online comments.

TOP TIP

Always make sure you make a note of where you get information from (your source). Keep it safely, as it can be very difficult later on to work out where it came from!

People as a source of information

If you want to get the most out of interviewing someone, or several people, you need to prepare carefully in advance.

The following points give some general advice about getting the most out of face-to-face interviews.

- Make sure you know what questions to ask to get the information you need.
- Explain why you want the information.
- Don't expect to be told confidential or sensitive information.
- Write clear notes so that you remember who told you what, and when. (See also page 62.)
- Note the contact details of the person you are interviewing and ask whether they mind if you contact them again should you think of anything later or need to clarify your notes.
- Thank them for their help.

If you want to ask a lot of people for their opinion, you may want to conduct a survey. You will need to design a questionnaire and analyse the results. This will be easier if you ask for **quantitative** responses – for example yes/no, true/false or ratings on a five-point scale – rather than opinions.

- Give careful thought to your representative sample (people whose opinions are relevant to the topic).
- Decide how many people to survey so that the results mean something.
- Keep the survey relatively short.

- Thank people who complete it.
- Analyse the results and write up your conclusions promptly.

TOP TIP

Test your questionnaire on volunteers before you 'go live' to check that there are no mistakes and the questions are easy to understand. Make any amendments before you conduct your 'real' survey.

Asking someone who knows a lot about a topic can be informative.

Avoiding pitfalls

Wikipedia is a good online source that covers many topics, and often in some depth. It is popular and free. However, it has an open-content policy, which means that anyone can contribute to and edit entries. People may post information whether it is correct or not. Wikipedia is moving towards greater checks on entries, but it is still sensible to check out information you find on this site somewhere else.

Apart from inaccuracy, there are other problems that you may find with any information you obtain through research, especially material found online.

- **Out-of-date material.** Check the date of everything and keep only the latest version of books, newspapers or magazines. Yesterday's news may be of little use if you are researching something topical.
- **Irrelevant details.** Often, only part of an article will be relevant to your search. For example, if you are forecasting future trends in an area of work, you do not need information about its history or related problems. When learners are struggling, they sometimes pad out answers with irrelevant information. If you've researched properly you can avoid this by having enough relevant information for your purposes.

- **Invalid assumptions.** This means someone has jumped to the wrong conclusion and made 2 + 2 = 5. You might do this if you see two friends chatting and think they are talking about you – whether they are or not! You can avoid problems in this area by double-checking your ideas and getting evidence to support them.

- **Bias.** This is when people hold strong views about a topic, or let their emotions or prejudices affect their judgement. An obvious example is asking a keen football fan for an objective evaluation of their team's performance!

- **Vested interests.** People may argue in a certain way because it's in their own interests to do so. For example, when the government said Home Information Packs must be prepared for all properties being sold, the Association of Home Information Pack Providers was in favour because it trains the people who prepare the packs. The National Association of Estate Agents and Royal Institution of Chartered Surveyors were not, because they thought they would lose business if people were put off selling their houses.

TOP TIP

Don't discard information that is affected by bias or vested interests. Just make it clear you know about the problem and have taken it into account.

Reading for a purpose

You may enjoy reading or you may find it tedious or difficult. If so, it helps to know that there are different ways to read, depending on what you're doing. For example, you wouldn't look for a programme in a TV guide in the same way that you would check an assignment for mistakes. You can save time and find information more easily if you use the best method of reading to suit your purpose. The following are some examples of ways of reading.

- **Skim reading** is used to check new information and get a general overview.
  To skim a book chapter, read the first and last paragraphs, the headings, subheadings and illustrations. It also helps to read the first sentence of each paragraph.

TOP TIP

News articles are written with the key points at the beginning, so concentrate on the first paragraph or two. Feature articles have a general introduction, and important information is contained in the main text.

- **Scanning** is used to see whether an article contains something you need – such as key words, dates or technical terms.
  Focus on capital or initial letters for a name, and figures for a date. Technical terms may be in bold or italics.

- **Light reading** is usually done for pleasure when you are relaxed, for example, reading a magazine article. You may not remember many facts afterwards, so this sort of reading isn't suitable for learning something or assessing its value.

- **Word-by-word reading (proofreading)** is important so that you don't miss anything, such as the dosage instructions for a strong medicine. You should proofread assignments before you submit them.

- **Reading for study (active reading)** means being actively involved so that you understand the information. It is rare to be naturally good at this, so you might have to work to develop this skill.

Developing critical and analytical skills

Developing critical and analytical skills involves looking at information for any flaws in the arguments. These skills are important when you progress to work or higher education (HE), so it's useful to practise them now on your BTEC Level 3 National course.

A useful technique for understanding, analysing, evaluating and remembering what you are reading is **SQ4R**.

SQ4R is an effective method. It consists of six steps.

1 Survey first, to get a general impression. Scan the information to see what it is about, when it was written and by whom. The source, and the reason it was written, may be important. Most newspapers, for example, have their own 'slant' that affects how information is presented.

2 Question your aims for reading this material. What are you hoping to find? What questions are you expecting it to answer?

3 Read the information three or four times. The first time, aim to get a general idea of the content. Use a dictionary to look up any new words. Then read more carefully to really understand what the writer means.

4 Respond by thinking critically about the information and how it relates to the topic you are studying. Does it answer your queries partially, fully or not at all? What information is factual and what is based on opinion? Is there evidence to support these opinions? Is there a reason why the author has taken this standpoint? Do you agree with it? How does it link to other information you have read? What is the opposite argument and is there any evidence to support this? Overall, how useful is this information?

5 Record the information by noting the key points. Use this to refresh your memory, if necessary, rather than re-reading the article.

6 Review your notes against the original to check you have included all important points. If you are also preparing a presentation, reviewing your notes will help you to remember key points more easily.

TOP TIP

SQ4R is just one method of reading for study. Research others and adapt them to suit your own style.

Taking good notes

There are many occasions when you need to take notes, such as when a visiting speaker is talking to your class. There's no point taking notes unless you write them in a way that will allow you to use them later.

Note-taking is a personal activity. Some people prefer to make diagrammatical sketches with key points in boxes linked by arrows, others prefer to write a series of bullet points. You will develop your own style, but the following hints and tips might help you at the start.

- Use A4 lined paper, rather than a notebook, so that you have more space and don't need to turn over so often.
- When you're reading for study, make sure you have a dictionary, pen, notepad and highlighter to hand.
- Leave a wide margin to record your own comments or queries.
- Put a heading at the top, such as the speaker's name and topic, as well as the date.
- If you are making notes from a book or an article, remember SQ4R and read it several times first. Your notes will only be effective if you understand the information.
- Don't write in complete sentences – it takes too long.
- Leave spaces for later additions or corrections.
- Use headings to keep your notes clear and well organised.
- Only write down relevant information, including key words and phrases.

- Highlight, underline or use capitals for essential points.
- Never copy chunks of text — always use your own words.
- Clearly identify quotations, and record your sources, so that you can cite them in your work. (Note the author's name, title, publisher, date and place of publication and the page number.)

TOP TIP

Make sure your information is accurate, up to date, relevant and valid. Be aware of bias, and don't confuse fact with opinion.

Key points

- Useful information may be verbal, printed, written, graphical or electronic.
- Effective research means knowing exactly what you are trying to find and where to look. Know how reference media are stored in your library and how to search online. Store important information carefully.
- Primary research is original data you obtain yourself. Secondary research is information prepared by someone else. If you use this, you must quote your sources in a bibliography.
- You can search for information by skimming and scanning, and read in different ways. Reading for study means actively involving yourself with the text, questioning what you are reading, and making notes to help your own understanding.
- Read widely around a topic to get different viewpoints. Don't accept everything you read as correct. Think about how it fits with other information you have obtained.
- Taking notes is a personal skill that takes time to develop. Start by using A4 lined pages with a margin, set out your notes clearly and label them. Only record essential information.

Action points

- Working with a friend, look back at the sources of information listed on page 58. For each type, identify examples of information relevant to your course that you could obtain from each source. See how many you can list under each type.
- Check your ability to find the information you need by answering each of the questions in **Activity: Finding information** on the next page. For any questions you get wrong, your first research task is to find out the correct answers as quickly as you can.
- Go to page 94 to find out how to access a website where you can check your ability to skim and scan information, improve your ability to differentiate fact from opinion, summarise text and much more.
- Check your ability to sort fact from opinion and spot vested interests by completing **Activity: Let's give you a tip...** on page 66. Check your ideas with the answers on page 93.

TOP TIP

Make a note of any information that you are struggling to understand so that you can discuss it with your tutor.

Activity: Finding information

Answer the following questions about finding information.

a) Four types of information that are available from the library in your centre, besides books, are:

1

2

3

4

b) When I visit the library, the way to check if a book I want is available is:

c) The difference between borrowing a book on short-term loan and on long-term loan is:

Short-term loan:

Long-term loan:

d) The journals that are stocked by the library that are relevant to my course include:

e) Useful information on the intranet at my centre includes:

f) Searchable databases and online magazines I can access include:

g) The quickest way to check if a book or journal contains the type of information I need is to:

h) The difference between a search engine, a portal, a directory site and a forum is:

i) Bookmarking useful websites means:

j) In addition to suggesting websites, Google can also provide the following types of information:

k) Specialist websites which provide useful information related to my course include:

l) Useful tips I would give to people starting on my course who need to find out information are:

Activity: Let's give you a tip...

In 2009, many businesses were struggling thanks to the credit crunch and falling consumer demand. Some, like Woolworths, closed down altogether. Others laid off staff, or announced wage cuts. Despite this, the government approved recommendations by the Low Pay Commission to increase the minimum wage rate from October. Although the rise was only small, many unions, including Unison and Usdaw, agreed it was better than a freeze, which had been wanted by the British Chambers of Commerce and the British Retail Consortium.

The government also announced new laws to stop restaurants and bars using tips to top up staff pay to the minimum level. *The Independent* newspaper claimed its 'fair tips, fair pay' campaign had won the day. It also reported that the British Hospitality Association was claiming this could result in up to 45,000 job losses. The Unite union also carried out a campaign, and its General Secretary claimed the decision a triumph for the poorly paid. Not everyone agreed. Some thought there should be no tipping at all, as in Australia. Others said the Canadian system was best – wages are low but generous tips are left, and this motivates staff to give excellent service.

a) Look at the table below. In your view, which of the statements are facts and which are opinions? In each case, justify your view.

Statement	Fact or opinion?	Justification
i) Having a national minimum wage helps low-paid workers.		
ii) Over one million people will benefit from the minimum wage increase.		
iii) The new law on tips will stop restaurants paying below minimum wage rates.		
iv) Using the Australian system of no tips would be better.		
v) The Canadian system guarantees good service.		
vi) 45,000 job losses will occur in the hospitality industry.		

b) All newspapers have their own way of putting forward the news. Go to page 94 to find out how to access a website which will help you to compare the way that news is reported in different newspapers.

Compare six different newspapers and make notes on:
i) the type of stories covered

ii) the way views are put forward

Activity: How to go about your research

For your project, you choose to design a roadside warning device that will alert a driver to an oncoming vehicle on a narrow road with a blind bend. Your tutor suggests it could be something like the solar powered speed warning signs that flash if you are driving too fast.

Use the spaces below to explain how you would go about researching information for your project.

Note, you do not have to include the actual research – just an overview of how you would carry out the process.

1 Types of information available to me

2 Planning my research

3 Primary and secondary research

4 People I will use as information sources

5 Pitfalls to avoid

6 How I will make a record of what I find out

7 The method I will follow when analysing the information I obtain

8 How I will bring it all together

TOP TIPS

The internet and other data sources are great, but with so much information out there how do you get to the important stuff? You need a research plan! Engineers are very good at planning.

Step Nine: Make an effective presentation

Case study: Well prepared presentations

Ryan is a very confident person who is never afraid to have a go if asked to do something completely new and out of his comfort zone. Most times he seems to get lucky, but when things go wrong it's usually big time – and quite a bit of effort is needed to recover the situation. Ryan's problem is that because he has a quick and agile brain he likes to get on with a task without first properly planning what he should be doing. In the first year of his BTEC Level 3 National in Engineering, he sometimes went off on the wrong track when carrying out experimental work because of his lack of preparation, or by not listening to instructions.

Ryan's ambition is to become a chartered engineer and to hold a senior position in a manufacturing business. He has an uncle who is the technical director of a company that manufactures the wing assemblies fitted to a new generation of wide-body passenger aircraft. The other day, Ryan and a colleague did a 10-minute 'What's your job' interview with his uncle as part of a research-gathering activity for a communications assignment.

'What surprised us was the amount of time a technical director spends making presentations to people. I thought the job just involved doing lots of calculations and making decisions about whether new designs will work or not.

'He told us that engineering is a very competitive business, and when you're trying to sell a new product to customers or are trying to raise cash from investors, you really do need to make first-class, well-prepared presentations. You've got to know your subject inside out, have confidence, and know how to deal honestly with questions you can't properly answer – watch *Dragons' Den* on television to see what I mean.'

Reflection points

Now think about your own presentation skills:

- Could you present an idea on a one-to-one basis to another learner? Could you present the same idea to a small group of colleagues?
- Given enough time to prepare, could you present your ideas to a much larger audience?
- Could you present to a group of people you don't know?

Making a presentation can be nerve-wracking. It involves several skills, including planning, preparation and communication. It tests your ability to work in a team, speak in public and use IT (normally PowerPoint). You also have to stay calm under pressure. However, as it is excellent practice for your future, you can expect presentations to be a common method of assessing your performance.

TOP TIP

When you're giving a presentation, keep to time, get to the point and use your time well.

Good planning and preparation

Being well prepared, and rehearsing beforehand, helps your confidence and your presentation. The following points will help you to do this.

- If you're part of a team, find out everyone's strengths and weaknesses and divide work fairly, taking these into account. Decide how long each person should speak, who should introduce the team and who will summarise at the end.

- Take into account the time you have been allocated, your resources and team skills. A simple, clear presentation is better – and safer – than a complicated one.

- If you're using PowerPoint, make slides more interesting by avoiding a series of bulleted lists and including artwork. Print PowerPoint notes for the audience. Use a fuller set of notes for yourself, as a prompt.

- Check the venue and time.

- Decide what to wear and check it's clean and presentable.

- Prepare, check and print your handouts.

- Decide, as a team, the order in which people will speak, bearing in mind the topic.

- Discuss possible questions and how to answer them.

- Rehearse beforehand to check your timings.

If you prepare properly, you can really enjoy giving a presentation.

TOP TIP

Rehearsing properly allows you to speak fluently, just glancing at your notes to remind you of the next key point.

On the day, you can achieve a better performance if you:

- arrive in plenty of time
- calm your nerves by taking deep breaths before going in front of your audience
- introduce yourself clearly, and smile at the audience
- avoid reading from your screen or your notes
- explain what you are going to do – especially if giving a demonstration – do it, and then review what you've done
- say you will deal with questions at the end of any demonstration
- answer questions honestly – don't exaggerate, guess or waffle
- respond positively to all feedback, which should be used to improve your performance next time.

TOP TIPS

Make sure you can be heard clearly by lifting your head and speaking a little more slowly and loudly than normal.

Key points

- When making a presentation, prepare well, don't be too ambitious, and have several rehearsals.
- When giving a demonstration, explain first what you are going to do and that you will answer questions at the end.

Case study: Learner quotes about making presentations

Most people start off feeling uncomfortable about talking in front of a group of people, whether you know them or not. This is what some real learners have said about having to give presentations as part of their BTEC course.

'I used to dread presentations on my course, but found that if I went through my notes again and again until I knew the presentation inside out, it made it much easier, and the presentations generally went well.'

Javinder, 17, BTEC Level 3 National in Construction

'I used to hate presenting to other people on my course, until I realised that most of them were as nervous about it as I was!'

Koichi, 21, BTEC Level 3 National in Art and Design

'Less is more! I used to rely on props and as I was nervous about forgetting things or running out of things to say I talked far too quickly. I had to repeat everything as nobody knew what I was on about! Some of my best presentations have been done without using slides or any other props at all, just talking (slowly of course) to my audience.'

Laura, 18, BTEC Level 3 National in Health & Social Care

'I used to be petrified of talking in front of other people but over time I've learned that, if I prepare well before a presentation, I usually feel much more confident on the day. If I know my material, I don't have to look down at my notes all the time and can make eye contact with the audience. Taking a few deep breaths before I begin keeps me calm and allows me to focus.'

Katie, 19, BTEC Level 3 National in Creative Media Production

'I prefer to be assessed by oral presentations as I'm dyslexic and my written work let's me down all the time. Everyone tells me that I really shine and show that I know my stuff when I present it to the rest of the group.'

Sam, 17, BTEC Level 3 National in Business

Activity: All right on the night?

Read the following account and answer the questions that follow.
If possible, compare ideas with a friend in your class.

Gemma looked around in exasperation. The team were on the final rehearsal of their presentation and nothing was going right. Amaya seemed to think it was funny. 'Honestly, Gemma, why don't you just chill for a bit?' she suggested. 'You know what they say – a bad dress rehearsal means we'll do really well tomorrow!'

Gemma glared at her. 'Well, can I make a suggestion, too, Amaya,' she retorted. 'Why don't you just concentrate for a change? Sprawling around and dissolving into giggles every five minutes isn't helping either.'

She turned to Adam. 'And I thought you were going to build a simple model,' she said, 'not one that falls apart every time you touch it.'

Adam looked crest fallen. 'But I wanted to show how it worked.'

'How it's supposed to work, you mean!' raged Gemma, all her worries and anxieties now coming to the fore. 'We'll look stupid if it ends up in bits on the floor tomorrow and Amaya just falls about laughing again.'

'And Imran,' continued Gemma, turning her sights on the last member of the team, 'why is it so difficult for you to count to three minutes? We've agreed over and over again we'll each talk for three minutes and every time you get carried away with the sound of your own voice and talk for twice as long. It just means we're going to overrun and get penalised. And stop trying to wriggle out of answering questions properly. For heaven's sake, if you don't know the answer, how hard is it just to say so?'

Silence fell. No one looked at each other. Adam fiddled with his model and something else fell off. Amaya wanted to laugh but didn't dare.

Imran was sulking and vowed never to say anything ever again. 'You wait,' he thought. 'Tomorrow I'll race through my part in one minute flat. And then what are you going to do?'

1 Identify the strengths and weaknesses of each member of the presentation team.

Name	Strengths	Weaknesses
Gemma		
Amaya		
Adam		
Imran		

2 What have the team done right, so far, in getting ready for their presentation?

3 Why do you think they are having problems?

4 If you were Gemma's tutor, what advice would you give her at this point?

Activity: Preparing your presentation

Ptek plc sells silver- and gold-plated snap-fit electrical connectors, manufactured using power presses and electrical-plating baths. The company has decided to make a presentation to the local residents' association about its 'green credentials', and why the discharge of waste water from the onsite treatment plant into a nearby a river is not a cause for concern.

You work for Ptek and will make the presentation using six PowerPoint slides as prompt cards. Use the spaces below to draft an overview of the content for each slide based on the following initial thoughts you've had: business good for local economy; health and safety compliance; EU legislation; waste directive (Defra); recycling; sound levels; HSE inspection.

3

4

5

6

Step Ten: Maximise your opportunities and manage your problems

Case study: Making the most of your opportunities

Emma is a second-year apprentice with a small hi-tech company that makes very expensive specialist sports cars. She is training to be a bodywork designer. Currently she's working with an aerodynamics engineer who is teaching her how to use simulation software that models the air-flow patterns over different body shapes. What kicked off her interest in this type of work was taking part in the Formula 1 challenge while still at school.

Rachel, the company's young and recently promoted chief engineer, has met with Emma to review her progress on the BTEC Level 3 Diploma in Aeronautical Engineering – and to update Emma's career development plan. Rachel told Emma to aim as high as possible, as there really is no limit to what you can achieve in the engineering business.

Rachel then told Emma something about her own background and how she had worked her way up to be chief engineer. After a difficult time at home, she left school at 16 with no qualifications and drifted around for several years doing dead-end jobs.

Her life was going nowhere until one day she met a friend who had just signed up on an access course at the local college. It sounded interesting and Rachel decided to give it a go. She was nervous about getting started and needed the help of a college counsellor to build up her confidence. A really helpful mentor, with a professional background in engineering, gave her a lot of support, and she went on to pass the course with excellent results.

During one lunch break at college, Rachel got talking to a group of trainee engineers who were taking BTEC First and Nationals. One of them arranged for her to visit their factory. The following September, Rachel enrolled on a BTEC Level 2 Diploma, and the rest is history.

'Have confidence in your abilities, and make the most of what's on offer. Really go for it, accept help when the going gets tough, accept that in life there are highs and lows, realise that effort brings rewards in the future' – that's Rachel's take on life and look where it's got her.

Reflection points

Do you have the confidence to make the best use of opportunities presented to you?

How do you tackle problems?

If your course takes one or two years to complete, then it is highly likely that you will experience some highs and lows in that time. You may find one or two topics harder than the rest. There may be distractions in your personal life to cope with. All of which means that you may not always be able to do your best.

It is, therefore, sensible to have an action plan to help you cope. It's also wise to plan how to make the best of opportunities for additional experiences or learning. This section shows you how to do this.

TOP TIP

Because life rarely runs smoothly, it's sensible to capitalise on the opportunities that come your way and have a plan to deal with problems.

Making the most of your opportunities

There will be many opportunities for learning on your course, not all of which will be in school or college. You should prepare for some of the following to maximise the opportunities that each offers.

- **External visits**. Prepare in advance by reading about relevant topics. Make notes when you are there. Write up your notes neatly and file them safely for future reference.

- **Visiting speakers**. Questions can usually be submitted to the speaker in advance. Think carefully about information that you would find helpful. Make notes, unless someone has been appointed to make notes for the whole group. You may be asked to thank the speaker on behalf of your group.

- **Work experience**. If work experience is an essential part of your course, your tutor will help you to organise your placement and tell you about the evidence you need to obtain. You may also get a special logbook in which to record your experiences. Read and re-read the units to which your evidence will apply, and make sure you understand the grading criteria and what you need to obtain. Make time to write up your notes, logbook and/or diary every night (if possible), while everything is fresh in your mind.

- **In your own workplace**. If you have a full-time or part-time job, watch for opportunities to find out more about relevant topics that relate to your course, such as health and safety, teamwork, dealing with customers, IT security and communications. Your employer will have had to address all of these issues. Finding out more about these issues will broaden your knowledge and give more depth to your assessment responses.

- **Television, newspapers, podcasts and other information sources**. The media can be an invaluable source of information. Look out for news bulletins relating to your studies, as well as information in topical television programmes – from *The Apprentice* to *Top Gear*. You can also read news headlines online (see page 67). Podcasts are useful, too. It will help if you know what topics you will be studying in the months to come, so you can spot useful opportunities as they arise.

TOP TIP

Remember that you can use online catch-up services, such as the BBC iPlayer or 4oD (for Channel 4 shows) to see TV programmes you have missed recently.

Minimising problems

Hopefully, any problems you experience during your course will only be minor, such as struggling to find an acceptable working method with someone in your team.

You should already know who to talk to about these issues, and who to go to if that person is absent or you would prefer to talk to someone else. If your problems are affecting your work, it's sensible to see your tutor promptly. It is a rare learner who is enthusiastic about every topic and gets on well with everyone else doing the course, so your tutor won't be surprised and will give you useful guidance (in confidence) to help.

TOP TIP

Don't delay talking to someone in confidence if you have a serious problem. If your course tutor is unavailable, talk to another staff member you like and trust instead.

Other sources of help

If you are unfortunate enough to have a more serious personal problem, the following sources of help may be available in your centre.

- **Professional counselling.** There may be a professional counselling service. If you see a counsellor, nothing you say during the session can be mentioned to another member of staff without your permission.

- **Complaint procedures.** If you have a serious complaint, the first step is to talk to your tutor. If you can't resolve your problem informally, there will be a formal learner complaint procedure. These procedures are used only for serious issues, not for minor difficulties.

- **Appeals procedures.** If you disagree with your final grade for an assignment, check the grading criteria and ask the subject tutor to explain how the grade was awarded. If you are still unhappy, talk to your personal tutor. If you still disagree, you have the right to make a formal appeal.

- **Disciplinary procedures.** These exist for when learners consistently flout a centre's rules, and ensure that all learners are dealt with in the same way. Hopefully, you will never get into trouble, but you should make sure that you read these procedures carefully to see what could happen if you did. Remember that being honest and making a swift apology is always the wisest course of action.

- **Serious illness.** Whether this involves you, a family member or a close friend, it could affect your attendance. Discuss the problem with your tutor promptly; you will be missing information from the first day you are absent. There are many solutions in this type of situation – such as sending notes by post and updating you electronically (providing you are well enough to cope with the work).

TOP TIP

It's important to know your centre's procedures for dealing with important issues such as complaints, major illnesses, learner appeals and disciplinary matters.

Key points

- Don't miss opportunities to learn more about relevant topics through external visits, listening to visiting speakers, work experience, being at work or even watching television.

- If you have difficulties or concerns, talk to your tutor, or another appropriate person, promptly to make sure your work isn't affected.

Action points

1 Prepare in advance to maximise your opportunities.
   a) List the opportunities available on your course for obtaining more information and talking to experts. You can check with your tutor to make sure you've identified them all.
   b) Check the content of each unit you will be studying so that you know the main topics and focus of each.
   c) Identify the information that may be relevant to your course on television, on radio, in newspapers and in podcasts.

2 Make sure you know how to cope if you have a serious problem.
   a) Check your centre's procedures so you know who to talk to in a crisis, and who to contact if that person is absent.
   b) Find out where you can get hold of a copy of the main procedures in your centre that might affect you if you have a serious problem. Then read them.

Activity: PMK Ltd

PMK Ltd uses injection-moulding machines to produce a range of small polymeric components in large batch sizes. The business has 10 moulding machines which are run on a 24/5 basis, with maintenance carried out at weekends when the machines are not being used. PMK employs a team of technicians to design, manufacture and commission the mould tools fitted to the injection machines.

PMK is a subcontractor to much larger companies, and it has to bid for contracts. Some examples of the types of products the company works on are rear light mouldings for cars, bathroom extractor fan bodies, telephone master sockets, shower heads, and body mouldings for power tools.

One of its competitors (Plasjec) is in financial difficulty, and the directors of PMK are considering a takeover bid. If the directors decide to go ahead, they will need to raise capital from a bank loan or share issue.

To raise capital for the takeover, the directors of PMK will present a business plan to the company's bank manager. Describe four important pieces of information which should be included in the plan.

If the takeover goes ahead, what issues will have to be addressed when considering the workforce and job roles?

Describe the expected economic benefits of merging the two companies.

AND FINALLY ...

Refer to this Study Skills Guide whenever you need to remind yourself about something related to your course. Keep it in a safe place so that you can use it whenever you need to refresh your memory. That way, you'll get the very best out of your course – and yourself!

TOP TIP

The time and effort you will be putting into this course deserve to be rewarded. Make sure you know how to confront and successfully overcome problems.

Skills building

This section has been written to help you improve the skills needed to do your best in your assignments. You may be excellent at some skills already, while others may need further work. The skills you can expect to demonstrate on your course include:

- your personal, learning and thinking skills (**PLTS**)
- your **functional skills** of ICT, maths/numeracy and English
- your proofreading and document production skills.

Personal, learning and thinking skills (PLTS)

These are the skills, personal qualities and behaviour that enable you to operate more independently, work more confidently with other people and be more effective at work. You'll develop these on your BTEC Level 3 National course through a variety of experiences and as you take on different roles and responsibilities.

The skills are divided into six groups.

1 **Independent enquirers** can process and evaluate information they investigate from different perspectives. They can plan what to do and how to do it, and take into account the consequences of making different decisions.

2 **Creative thinkers** generate and explore different ideas. They make connections between ideas, events and experiences that enable them to be inventive and imaginative.

3 **Reflective learners** can assess themselves and other people. They can evaluate their own strengths and limitations. They set themselves realistic goals, monitor their own performance and welcome feedback.

4 **Team workers** collaborate with other people to achieve common goals. They are fair and considerate to others, whether as a team leader or team member, and take account of different opinions.

5 **Self-managers** are well-organised and show personal responsibility, initiative, creativity and enterprise. They look for new challenges and responsibilities, and are flexible when priorities change.

6 **Effective participators** play a full part in the life of their school, college, workplace or wider community by taking responsible action to bring improvements for others as well as themselves.

Action points

1 Many parts of this Study Skills Guide relate to the development of your own personal, learning and thinking skills. For each of the following, suggest the main skill groups to which the chapter relates. Refer to the box above and write a number next to each chapter title below.

a) Use your time wisely. ____

b) Understand how to research and analyse information. ____

c) Work productively as a member of a group. ____

d) Understand yourself. ____

e) Utilise all your resources. ____

f) Maximise your opportunities and manage your problems. ____

2 You have been on your BTEC National course for a few months now and, although everyone is enjoying the work, you realise that some of the learners have complaints.

First, several learners object to an increase in the price of printouts and photocopying, on the basis that they can't do good work for their assignments if this is too expensive. You disagree and think that the prices are reasonable, given the cost of paper.

Second, a timetable change means your 2 pm – 4 pm Friday afternoon class has been moved to 9 am – 11 am. Some learners are annoyed and want it changed back, while others are delighted.

a) For the first problem, identify four factors which could indicate that those complaining about the price rise might be justified.

1

2

3

4

b) Now consider the second problem.

   i) Think about which learners in your group would be most affected by the timetable change. Who might be most disturbed? Who might benefit from the earlier start?

   ii) Try to think of a creative solution, or compromise, that would please both groups.

c) During the discussions about these issues, some quieter members of the class are often shouted down by the more excitable members. Suggest a strategy for dealing with this which everyone is likely to accept.

You can also check your ideas with the suggestions given on page 93.

3 a) Complete the chart opposite, identifying occasions when you may need to demonstrate personal, learning and thinking skills in your future career. Alternatively, apply each area to a part-time job you are currently doing.

   b) Identify areas where you think you are quite strong and put a tick in the 'S' column. Check that you could provide evidence to support this judgement, such as a time when you have demonstrated this skill.

   c) Now consider areas where you are not so good and put a cross in the 'W' column.

   d) Then practise self-management by identifying two appropriate goals to achieve over the next month and make a note of them in the space provided. If possible, talk through your ideas at your next individual tutorial.

Personal, learning and thinking skills for future career/current part-time job				
Skill group	**Example skills**	**Occasions when you use/ will use skill**	**S**	**W**
Independent enquirers	Finding information Solving problems Making decisions Reconciling conflicting information or views Justifying decisions			
Creative thinkers	Finding imaginative solutions Making original connections Finding new ways to do something Opportunities for being innovative and inventive			
Reflective learners	Goals you may set yourself Reviewing your own progress Encouraging feedback Dealing with setbacks or criticism			
Team workers	Working with others Coping with different views to your own Adapting your behaviour Being fair and considerate			
Self-managers	Being self-starting and showing initiative Dealing positively with changing priorities Organising your own time and resources Dealing with pressure Managing your emotions			
Effective participators	Identifying issues of concern to others Proposing ways forward Identifying improvements for others Influencing other people Putting forward a persuasive argument			
Goals	1			
	2			

Functional skills

Functional skills are practical skills that everyone needs to have in order to study and work effectively. They involve using and applying English, maths and ICT.

Improving your literacy skills

Your written English communication skills

A good vocabulary increases your ability to explain yourself clearly. Work that is presented without spelling and punctuation errors looks professional and increases the likelihood of someone understanding your intended meaning. Your written communication skills will be tested in many assignments. You should work at improving areas of weakness, such as spelling, punctuation or vocabulary.

Try the following ideas to help you improve your written communication skills.

- Read more as this introduces you to new words, and it will help your spelling.

- Look up new words in a dictionary and try to use them in conversation.

- Use a thesaurus (you can access one electronically in Word) to find alternatives to words you use a lot; this adds variety to your work.

- Never use words you don't understand in the hope that they sound impressive.

- Write neatly, so people can read what you've written.

- Do crosswords to improve your word power and spelling.

- Improve your punctuation – especially the use of apostrophes – either by using an online program or a communication textbook.

- Go to page 94 to find out how to gain access to some helpful websites for this section.

Verbal and non-verbal communication (NVC) skills

Talking appropriately means using the right words and 'tone'; using the right body language means sending positive signals to reinforce this message – such as smiling at someone when you say hello. Both verbal and non-verbal communication skills are essential when dealing with people at work.

The following ideas are some hints for successful communication.

- Be polite, tactful and sensitive to other people's feelings.

- Think about the words and phrases that you like to hear, and use them when communicating with other people.

- Use simple language so that people can understand you easily. Explain what you mean, when necessary.

- Speak at the right pace. Don't speak so slowly that everyone loses interest, or so fast that no one can understand you.

- Speak loudly enough for people to hear you clearly – but don't shout!

- Think about the specific needs of different people – whether you are talking to a senior manager, an important client, a shy colleague or an angry customer.

- Recognise the importance of non-verbal communication (NVC) so that you send positive signals by smiling, making eye contact, giving an encouraging nod or leaning forwards to show interest.

- Read other people's body language to spot if they are anxious or impatient so that you can react appropriately.

TOP TIP

Make sure you use the right tone for the person you're talking to. Would you talk to an adult in the same way you'd talk to a very young child?

Action points

1 Go to page 94 to find out how to gain access to websites which can help you to improve your literacy skills.

2 A battery made in China contained the following information.

> **DO NOT CONNECT IMPROPERLY**
>
> **CHARGE OR DISPOSE OF IN FIRE**

a) Can you see any problems with this? Give a reason for your answer.

b) Reword the information so that it is unambiguous.

3 If you ever thought you could completely trust the spellchecker on your computer, type the text given in box A on the next page into your computer. Your spellchecker will not highlight a single error; yet even at a glance you should be able to spot dozens of errors!

Read the passage in box A and try to understand it. Then rewrite it in box B on the next page without spelling, grammatical or punctuation errors. Compare your finished work with the suggested version on page 93.

Box A

Anyone desirable to write books or reports, be they short or long, should strive too maximise they're optimal use of one's English grammar and obliviously there is an need for correct spelling two one should not neglect punctuation neither.

Frequent lea, many people and individuals become confusing or just do not no it, when righting, when words that mean different, when sounding identically, or when pronounced very similar, are knot too bee spelled inn the same whey. The quay two suck seeding is dew care, a lack off witch Leeds too Miss Spellings that mite otherwise of bean a voided. Spell chequers donut find awl missed takes.

Despite all the pitfalls how ever, with practise, patients and the right altitude, any one can soon become a grate writer and speaker, as what I did.

Box B Now rewrite the passage in the space below without errors.

4 In each of the statements listed in the table below, suggest what the body language described might mean.

Statement	What might this body language mean?
a) You are talking to your manager when he steps away from you and crosses his arms over his chest.	
b) You are talking to your friend about what she did at the weekend but she's avoiding making eye contact with you.	
c) During a tutorial session, your tutor is constantly tapping his fingers on the arm of his chair.	
d) Whenever you talk to your friend about your next assignment, she bites her lower lip.	

Improving your maths or numeracy skills

If you think numeracy isn't relevant to you, then think again! Numeracy is an essential life skill. If you can't carry out basic calculations accurately then you will have problems, perhaps when you least expect them. You'll often encounter numbers in various contexts – sometimes they will be correctly given, sometimes not. Unless you have a basic understanding of numeracy, you won't be able to tell the difference.

Good numeracy skills will improve your ability to express yourself, especially in assignments and at work. If you have problems, there are strategies that you can practise to help:

- Try to do basic calculations in your head, then check them on a calculator.
- Ask your tutor for help if important calculations give you problems.
- When you are using your computer, use the onscreen calculator (or a spreadsheet package) to do calculations.
- Investigate puzzle sites and brain-training software, such as Dr Kageyama's Maths Training by Nintendo.

Action points

1 Go to page 94 to find out how to gain access to websites which can help you to improve your numeracy skills.

2 Try the following task with a friend or family member:

Each of you should write down 36 simple calculations in a list, eg

8×6, $19 - 8$, $14 + 6$.

Exchange lists. See who can answer the most calculations correctly in the shortest time.

3 Figures aren't always what they appear to be. For example, Sophie watches *Who Wants To Be a Millionaire?* She hears Chris Tarrant say

that there have been over 500 shows, with 1200 contestants who have each won over £50,000 on average. Five people have won £1 million.

Sophie says she is going to enter because she is almost certain to win more than £50,000 and could even win a million pounds.

a) On the figures given, what is the approximate total of money won over 500 shows (to the nearest £ million)?

b) Assuming that Sophie is chosen to appear on the show, and makes it on air as a contestant, do you think Sophie's argument that she will 'almost certainly' win more than £50,000 is correct? Give a reason for your answer.

(The correct answer is on page 94.)

4 You have a part-time job and have been asked to carry out a survey on the usage of the drinks vending machine. You decide to survey 500 people, and find that:
- 225 use the machine to buy one cup of coffee per day only
- 100 use the machine to buy one cup of tea per day only
- 75 use the machine to buy one cup of cold drink per day only
- 50 use the machine to buy one cup of hot chocolate per day only
- the rest are non-users
- the ratio of male to female users is 2:1.

a) How many men in your survey use the machine?

b) How many women in your survey use the machine?

c) Calculate the proportion of the people in your survey that use the machine.

Express this as a fraction and as a percentage.

d) What is the ratio of coffee drinkers to tea drinkers in your survey?

e) What is the ratio of coffee drinkers to hot chocolate drinkers in your survey?

f) If people continue to purchase from the machine in the same ratio found in your survey, and last month 1800 cups of coffee were sold, what would you expect the sales of the cold drinks to be?

g) Using the answer to f), if coffee costs 65p and all cold drinks cost 60p, how much would have been spent in total last month on these two items?

Improving your ICT skills

Good ICT skills are an asset in many aspects of your daily life, and not just for those studying to be IT practitioners.

These are ways in which you can improve your ICT skills.

- Check that you can use the main features of the software packages you need to produce your assignments, eg Word, Excel and PowerPoint.

- Choose a good search engine and learn to use it properly. For more information, go to page 94 to find out how to access a useful website.

- Developing and using your IT skills enables you to enhance your assignments. This may include learning how to import and export text and artwork from one package to another, taking digital photographs and inserting them into your work, and/or creating drawings or diagrams by using appropriate software.

Action points

1 Check your basic knowledge of IT terminology by identifying each of these items on your computer screen:

a) taskbar	**f)** scroll bars
b) toolbar	**g)** status bar
c) title bar	**h)** insertion point
d) menu bar	**i)** maximise/
e) mouse pointer	minimise button.

2 Assess your IT skills by identifying the packages and operations you find easy to use and those that you find more difficult. If you use Microsoft Office products (Word, PowerPoint, Access or Excel) you can find out more about improving your skills online. Go to page 94 to find out how to access a useful website for this action points section.

3 Search the internet to find a useful dictionary of IT terms. Bookmark it for future use. Find out the meaning of any of the following terms that you don't know already:

a) portal

b) cached link

c) home page

d) browser

e) firewall

f) HTML

g) URL

h) cookie

i) hyperlink

j) freeware.

Proofreading and document preparation skills

Improving your keyboard, document production and general IT skills can save you hours of time. When you have good skills, the work you produce will be of a far more professional standard.

- Think about learning to touch-type. Your centre may have a workshop you can join, or you can use an online program – go to page 94 to find out how you can access websites that will allow you to test and work on improving your typing skills.

- Obtain correct examples of any document formats you will have to use, such as a report or summary, either from your tutor, the internet or from a textbook.

- Proofread all your work carefully. A spellchecker won't find all your mistakes, so you must read through it yourself as well.

- Make sure your work looks professional by using a suitable typeface and font size, as well as reasonable margins.

- Print your work and store the printouts neatly, so that it stays in perfect condition for when you hand it in.

Action points

1 You can check and improve your typing skills using online typing sites – see link in previous section.

2 Check your ability to create documents by scoring yourself out of 5 for each of the following questions, where 5 is something you can do easily and 0 is something you can't do at all. Then focus on improving every score where you rated yourself 3 or less.

I know how to:

a) create a new document and open a saved document _____

b) use the mouse to click, double-click and drag objects _____

c) use drop-down menus _____

d) customise my toolbars by adding or deleting options _____

e) save and/or print a document _____

f) create folders and sub-folders to organise my work _____

g) move a folder I use regularly to My Places _____

h) amend text in a document _____

i) select, copy, paste and delete information in a document _____

j) quickly find and replace text in a document _____

k) insert special characters _____

l) create a table or insert a diagram in a document _____

m) change the text size, font and colour _____

n) add bold, italics or underscore _____

o) create a bullet or numbered list _____

p) align text left, right or centred _____

q) format pages before they are printed _____

r) proofread a document so that there are no mistakes _____.

Answers

Activity: Let's give you a tip... (page 66)

a) i) Fact

ii) Opinion – the number cannot be validated

iii) Fact

iv) Opinion

v) Opinion

vi) Opinion – again the number is estimated

Skills building answers

PLTS action points (page 83)

1 a) Use your time wisely = **5** Self-managers

b) Understand how to research and analyse information = **1** Independent enquirers, **5** Self-managers

c) Work productively as a member of a group = **4** Team workers, **6** Effective participators

d) Understand yourself = **3** Reflective learners

e) Utilise all your resources = **5** Self-managers

f) Maximise your opportunities and manage your problems = **1** Independent enquirers, **2** Creative thinkers, **3** Reflective learners, **5** Self-managers

2 a) Factors to consider in relation to the increased photocopying/printing charges include: the comparative prices charged by other schools/colleges, how often there is a price rise, whether any printing or photocopying at all can be done without charge, whether there are any concessions for special tasks or assignments, the availability of class sets of books/popular library books for loan (which reduces the need for photocopying).

b) i) An earlier start will be more likely to negatively affect those who live further away and who are reliant on public transport, particularly in rural areas. The earlier finish will benefit anyone who has a part-time job that starts on a Friday afternoon or who has after-college commitments such as looking after younger sisters or brothers.

ii) The scope for compromise would depend on whether there are any classes between 11 am and 2 pm on a Friday, whether tutors had any flexibility, and whether the new 9 am – 11 am class could be moved to another time or day.

c) One strategy would be to allow discussion for a set time, ensure everyone had spoken, then put the issue to a vote. The leader should prompt suggestions from quieter members by asking people individually what they think.

Literacy skills action points (page 87)

2 a) The statement reads as if it is acceptable to either charge it or dispose of it in fire.

b) Do not connect this battery improperly. Do not recharge it and do not dispose of it in fire.

3 Anyone who wishes to write books or reports, whether short or long, should try to use English grammatically. Obviously there is a need for correct spelling, too. Punctuation should also not be neglected.

Frequently, people confuse words with different meanings when they are writing, especially when these sound identical or very similar, even when they must not be spelled in the same way. The key to succeeding is due care, a lack of which leads to mis-spellings that might otherwise have been avoided. Spellcheckers do not find all mistakes.

Despite all the pitfalls, however, with practice, patience and the right attitude, anyone can soon become a great writer and speaker, like me.

4 Possible answers.

a) Stepping backwards and crossing arms across the chest might indicate that your manager is creating a barrier between you and himself. This may be because he is angry with you.

b) Your friend may be feeling guilty about what she did at the weekend, or not confident that you will approve of what she tells you.

c) Your tutor might be frustrated as he has many things to do and so wants the tutorial to finish quickly.

d) Your friend might be anxious about the next assignment or about the time she has to complete it.

Numeracy action points (page 90)

3 a) £60 million

b) Sophie's argument is incorrect as £50,000 is an average, some contestants will win more, but many will win much less. The distribution of prize money is greater at lower amounts because more people win small amounts of money than large amounts – and only five contestants have won the top prize of £1 million.

4 a) 300

b) 150

c) 9/10ths, 90%

d) 225:100 (= 45:20) = 9:4

e) 225:50 = 9:2

f) 600

g) £1530

Accessing website links

Links to various websites are referred to throughout this BTEC Level 3 National Study Skills Guide. To ensure that these links are up to date, that they work and that the sites aren't inadvertently linked to any material that could be considered offensive, we have made the links available on our website: www.pearsonhotlinks.co.uk. When you visit the site, search by either the title BTEC Level 3 National Study Skills Guide in Engineering or ISBN 9781846905599. From here you can gain access to the website links and information on how they can be used to help you with your studies.

Useful terms

Accreditation of Prior Learning (APL)
Some of your previous achievements and experiences may be able to be used to count towards your qualification.

Apprenticeships
Schemes that enable you to work and earn money at the same time as you gain further qualifications (an NVQ award and a technical certificate) and improve your functional skills. Apprentices learn work-based skills relevant to their job role and their chosen industry. See page 94 for information on how to access a website where you can find out more.

Assessment methods
Techniques used to check that your work demonstrates the learning and understanding required for your qualification, such as assignments, case studies and practical tasks.

Assessor
An assessor is the tutor who marks or assesses your work.

Assignment
A complex task or mini-project set to meet specific grading criteria and learning outcomes.

Awarding body
An organisation responsible for devising, assessing and issuing qualifications. The awarding body for all BTEC qualifications is Edexcel.

Credit value
The number of credits attached to your BTEC course. The credit value increases in relation to the length of time you need to complete the course, from 30 credits for a BTEC Level 3 Certificate, 60 credits for a Subsidiary Diploma, 120 credits for a Diploma, up to 180 credits for an Extended Diploma.

Degrees
Higher education qualifications offered by universities and colleges. Foundation degrees take two years to complete; honours degrees may take three years or longer.

Department for Business Innovation and Skills (BIS)
BIS is responsible for further and higher education

and skills training, as well as functions related to trade and industry. See page 94 for information on how to access a website where you can find out more.

Department for Education
The Department for Education is responsible for schools and education, as well as for children's services. See page 94 for information on how to access a website where you can find out more.

Distance learning
When you learn and/or study for a qualification at home or at work. You communicate with your tutor and/or the centre that organises the course by post, telephone or electronically.

Educational Maintenance Award (EMA)
An EMA is a means-tested award that provides eligible learners under 19 who are studying a full-time course at school or college with a cash sum of money every week. See page 94 for information on how to access a website where you can find out more.

External verification
Formal checking of the programme by an Edexcel representative that focuses on sampling various assignments to check content, accurate assessment and grading.

Forbidden combinations
There are some qualifications that cannot be taken simultaneously because their content is too similar.

Functional skills
Practical skills in English, maths and ICT that enable people to work confidently, effectively and independently. Level 2 Functional Skills are mapped to the units of BTEC Level 3 National qualifications. They aren't compulsory to achieve on the course, but are of great use.

Grade boundaries
Pre-set points that determine whether you will achieve a pass, merit or distinction as the overall final grade(s) for your qualification.

Grading criteria
The specific evidence you have to demonstrate to obtain a particular grade in the unit.

Grading domains

The main areas of learning that support the learning outcomes. On a BTEC Level 3 National course these are: application of knowledge and understanding; development of practical and technical skills; personal development for occupational roles; application of PLTS and functional skills.

Grading grid

The table in each unit of your qualification specification that sets out what you have to show you can do.

Higher education (HE)

Post-secondary and post-further education, usually provided by universities and colleges.

Higher-level skills

These are skills such as evaluating or critically assessing information. They are more difficult than lower-level skills such as writing a description or making a list. You must be able to demonstrate higher-level skills to achieve a distinction.

Indicative reading

Recommended books and journals whose content is both suitable and relevant for the BTEC unit studied.

Induction

A short programme of events at the start of a course designed to give you essential information and introduce you to your fellow learners and tutors, so that you can settle down as quickly and easily as possible.

Internal verification

The quality checks carried out by nominated tutors at your school or college to ensure that all assignments are at the right level and cover appropriate learning outcomes and grading criteria, and that all assessors are marking work consistently and to the same standard.

Investors in People (IiP)

A national quality standard that sets a level of good practice for training and developing people within a business. Participating organisations must demonstrate commitment to achieve the standard.

Learning outcomes

The knowledge and skills you must demonstrate to show that you have effectively learned a unit.

Learning support

Additional help that is available to all learners in a school or college who have learning difficulties or other special needs.

Levels of study

The depth, breadth and complexity of knowledge, understanding and skills required to achieve a qualification, which also determines its level. Level 2 equates to GCSE level, and Level 3 equates to A-level. As you successfully achieve one level, you can then progress to the next. BTEC qualifications are offered at Entry Level, then Levels 1, 2, 3, 4 and 5.

Local Education Authority (LEA)

The local government body responsible for providing education for all learners of compulsory school age. The LEA is also responsible for managing the education budget for 16–19-year-old learners in its area.

Mandatory units

These are units that all learners must complete to gain a qualification, in this case a BTEC Level 3 National. Some BTEC qualifications have an overarching title, eg Construction, but within Construction you can choose different pathways. Your chosen pathway may have additional mandatory units specific to that pathway.

Mentor

A more experienced person who will guide you and counsel you if you have a problem or difficulty.

Mode of delivery

The way in which a qualification is offered to learners, for example part-time, full-time, as a short course or by distance learning.

National Occupational Standard (NOS)

Statements of the skills, knowledge and understanding you need to develop in order to be competent at a particular job.

National Vocational Qualification (NVQ)

Qualifications that concentrate on the practical skills and knowledge required to do a job competently. They are usually assessed in the workplace and range from Level 1 (the lowest) to Level 5 (the highest).

Nested qualifications

Qualifications that have common units, so that learners can easily progress from one to another by adding on more units

Ofqual
The public body responsible for regulating qualifications, exams and tests in England.

Optional units
Units on your course from which you may be able to make a choice. They help you specialise your skills, knowledge and understanding, and may help progression into work or further education.

Pathway
All BTEC Level 3 National qualifications comprise a small number of mandatory units and a larger number of optional units. These units are grouped into different combinations to provide alternative pathways to achieving the qualification. These pathways are usually linked to different career preferences.

Peer review
This involves feedback on your performance by your peers (members of your team or class group.) You will also be given an opportunity to review their performance.

Plagiarism
The practice of copying someone else's work or work from any other sources (eg the internet), and passing it off as your own. This practice is strictly forbidden on all courses.

Personal, learning and thinking skills (PLTS)
The skills, personal qualities and behaviour that improve your ability to work independently. Developing these skills makes you more effective and confident at work. Opportunities for developing these skills are a feature of all BTEC Level 3 National courses. These skills aren't compulsory to achieve on the course, but are of great use to you.

Portfolio
A collection of work compiled by a learner, usually as evidence of learning, to present to an assessor.

Procrastinator
Someone who is forever putting off or delaying work, either because they are lazy or because they have poor organisational skills.

Professional body
An organisation that exists to promote or support a particular profession, such as the Royal Institute of British Architects (RIBA).

Professional development and training
This involves undertaking activities relevant to your job to increase and/or update your knowledge and skills.

Project
A project is a comprehensive piece of work which normally involves original research and investigation by an individual or by a team. The findings and results may be presented in writing and summarised as a presentation.

Qualifications and Credit Framework (QCF)
The QCF is a framework for recognising skills and qualifications. It does this by awarding credit for qualifications and units so that they are easier to measure and compare. All BTEC Level 3 National qualifications are part of the QCF.

Qualifications and Curriculum Development Agency (QCDA)
The QCDA is responsible for maintaining and developing the national curriculum, delivering assessments, tests and examinations, and reforming qualifications.

Quality assurance
In education, this is the process of continually checking that a course of study is meeting the specific requirements set down by the awarding body.

Sector Skills Councils (SSCs)
The 25 employer-led, independent organisations responsible for improving workforce skills in the UK by identifying skill gaps and improving learning in the workplace. Each council covers a different type of industry.

Semester
Many universities and colleges divide their academic year into two halves or semesters, one from September to January and one from February to July.

Seminar
A learning event involving a group of learners and a tutor, which may be learner-led and may follow research into a topic that has been introduced at an earlier stage.

Study buddy
A person in your group or class who takes notes for you and keeps you informed of important developments if you are absent. You do the same for them in return.

Time-constrained assignment

An assessment you must complete within a fixed time limit.

Tutorial

An individual or small group meeting with your tutor at which you can discuss your current work and other more general course issues. At an individual tutorial, your progress on the course will be discussed and you can raise any concerns or personal worries you may have.

The University and Colleges Admissions Service (UCAS)

UCAS (pronounced 'you-cass') is the central organisation that processes all applications for higher education (HE) courses.

UCAS points

The number of points allocated by UCAS for the qualifications you have obtained. Higher education institutions specify how many points you need to be accepted on the courses they offer. Go to page 94 for information on how to access a website where you can find out more.

Unit abstract

The summary at the start of each BTEC unit that tells you what the unit is about.

Unit content

Details about the topics covered by the unit and the knowledge and skills you need to complete it.

Unit points

The number of points you gain when you complete a unit. These will depend on the grade you achieve (pass, merit or distinction).

Vocational qualification

Designed to develop knowledge and understanding relevant to a chosen area of work.

Work experience

Time you spend on an employer's premises when you learn about the enterprise, carry out work-based tasks and develop skills and knowledge.

Please note that all information given within these useful terms was correct at the time of going to press.